Memories in Melody

Memories in Melody

A lifetime of personal experiences
from the golden era of popular music
by a legendary broadcaster

Jack Ellsworth

Text © 2012 Jack Ellsworth
All Rights Reserved
The text and photos from author Jack Ellsworth's private collection in this book remain the copyright of the author.

All rights reserved. No part of this book may be used or reproduced in any manner whatsoever without written permission, except in the case of brief excerpts embodied in articles or reviews.

Published 2012
Memories in Melody
by Jack Ellsworth (Shiebler)

ISBN-13: 978-1481100786
ISBN-10: 1481100785

Edited by Susan Elise Shiebler
Additional editing and assistance: Ruth Shiebler, Lois Mitchell, Dorothy Shiebler, Michael Mingino, Elissa Mingino, Matthew Mingino, Christa Mingino, Katanya Carson and Suzanne Ahern
Cover Design: Susan Elise Shiebler, Matthew Mingino, Suzanne Ahern

*To my darling wife Dot,
without whom
nothing in my life
would have been possible,
I love you.*

Contents

Dedication	v
Contents	vii-ix
Acknowledgments	1
Foreword	5

Part I: The Early Years — 7

1 Childhood	11
2 New York As it Was	19
3 The Marines	25

Part II: The Next Fifty Years   33

  4 Providence   39
  5 Meeting Dot   57
  6 WALK and WLIM   65
  7 Family and Faith   79

Part III: Famous Friends   95
Photo Collection   96

  8 Gary Cooper   127
  9 Buddy Clark   131
10 Dick Powell   135
11 Benny Goodman   151
12 Remembering Benny Goodman's Carnegie Hall Concert   165
13 Glenn Miller   173
14 Bing Crosby   181
15 Tommy Dorsey   195
16 Ella Fitzgerald   203
17 Fred Astaire   207
18 P.G. Wodehouse   213
19 Frank Sinatra   219
20 Count Basie   233
21 Christmas Music and Memories   239
22 Stories from the Stars   249

Part IV: Acclaim and Recognition   253

23 The Silver Fox   255
24 Memories in Melody   257
25 Jack Ellsworth to be Honored   261
26 Paul Harvey   265
27 WLIM Tribute   267
28 Jack Ellsworth is Back   269

Part V: Recollections   273

29 Whatever Happened To...?   275
30 Radio Recollections   281

Acknowledgements

I would like to thank all those directly and indirectly involved in the preparation of this book:

Thank you to my wife Dot for starting years ago to type and transfer my various newspaper columns to Word documents on the computer. I am so thankful to her, not only for her work, but for her support in helping me to fulfill this dream.

Thank you to my sons Gary, Glenn, our "adopted" son, Ed and our beautiful daughters-in-law, Linda, Marilyn and Nancy.

I would like to thank author Dick Grudens for his continued friendship and loyalty.

My deepest thanks to Dr. Joseph Harder who, through his prayers, wisdom and support, has helped to guide our family through many of life's twists and turns.

Much gratitude and respect to photographer, Jim Mooney who has been there for decades, capturing all of the special personal and professional moments in my life.

My sincere gratefulness to my dear sister Ruth for her tremendous support and assistance throughout this entire process.

My deepest gratitude to everyone at WALK radio for their continued support.

To my granddaughters, Elissa, and Christa who sat with me while we worked on the book. I thank them also for introducing me to "YouTube" where I have been able to become reacquainted with all of the stars/friends in this book and add to my knowledge!

Thank you to my grandsons, Matthew and Michael, who in the last few years have helped me on the air fulfilling my dream to continue the "Memories in Melody" legacy.

My sincere gratitude to Larry O'Brien for his friendship, and for his time and enthusiasm in writing the foreword.

Most of all, I am deeply grateful to my daughter Susan for suggesting the idea for this book and for helping me publish it. I'd like to thank her for the endless hours going through my archives, compiling photos, taking my dictation, and finally editing and designing the layout. We spent many long hours, day and night, and I enjoyed our time working together so much.

Special gratitude and acknowledgement to Kathryn Crosby, Barbara Sinatra, Doris Day, the families of Gary Cooper, Buddy Clark, Fred Astaire, Dick Powell, Benny Goodman, Glenn Miller, Ella Fitzgerald, Tommy Dorsey, P.G. Wodehouse, Frank Sinatra, Count Basie, Eubie Blake, Louis Armstrong, Johnny Mince, Perry Como, Percy Faith and Arthur Tracy.

Additional thanks for quotes from: jazz critic, Richard Sudhalter, Norman Grantz, Red Norvo, Dick Haymes, Will Friedwald, Gene Kelly, Ken Barnes, Danny Quatrochi and for excerpts and contributions from Dick Grudens, Paul Harvey, Rick Hall, Chuck Anderson, Betty Jane Welgand and Brian Curry. Thank you to the Long Island Advance and to Terry Tuthill for his support and for always following my career.

My sincere gratitude to all of my many sponsors over the years. Thank you for your support, for trusting us and for believing in us for so long!

Last but never least, I would like to express my heartfelt gratitude to my devoted radio listeners, especially those who have followed me these many years. Without an audience, there is no show, without my listeners, there would be no way to share the music. You have not only been fans but also friends and the latter has meant so much more.

~Jack Ellsworth
  December 2012

Larry O'Brien and Jack Ellsworth - 1983
(Jack Ellsworth collection)

(top)With famous Glenn Miller orchestra leader and good friend Larry O'Brien in 1983 (bottom) In 2007 with Larry and my grandson Matthew (who is now 17 and on the air with me!) at the Patchogue Theatre for a concert featuring Larry's superb direction of the world famous Glenn Miller orchestra.

Foreword

When I was asked to write the foreword for "Memories in Melody" by Jack Ellsworth, my main concern was properly addressing the vast and comprehensive knowledge of "40's music" that Jack calls on, knowledge that goes deep into the roots of the era.

When I did my first interview with Jack, he suggested a few ballads of which I had been unaware, one being "I'm Thrilled." This was the "intro" to the treasure of music in our Glenn Miller Orchestra library. One of the keys of exploring this wealth was listening to the suggestions from my friend Jack and seeing the delight on the faces when we played them on Long Island!

I am one of the many who have benefitted from the knowledge that Jack has shared through the years. Folks on Long Island are fortunate to still have Jack three days a week on the air. For the last 65 years, he has provided quality music and insights to Long Islanders which have brightened days and added pleasure to countless loyal fans. They wouldn't miss Jack's show and the joy he brings to their lives. I'm sure you'll enjoy <u>reading</u> about Jack almost as much as <u>hearing</u> the treasures and anecdotes he brings over the airwaves.

One final note, his partner, wife and "co-pilot" Dot, has played a a huge part in his career. Her assistance and support have been invaluable to him.
From all of us who know her, Thanks Dotty!
and...

Thanks Jack,

Larry O'Brien
Former Musical Director (25 years) of the Glenn Miller Orchestra
(Now retired with wife Judy in Hawaii)

Part I

The Early Years

Ellsworth Adee Shiebler, 1923

With my mother Dorothy, my sister Ruth, and brother Larry, 1933

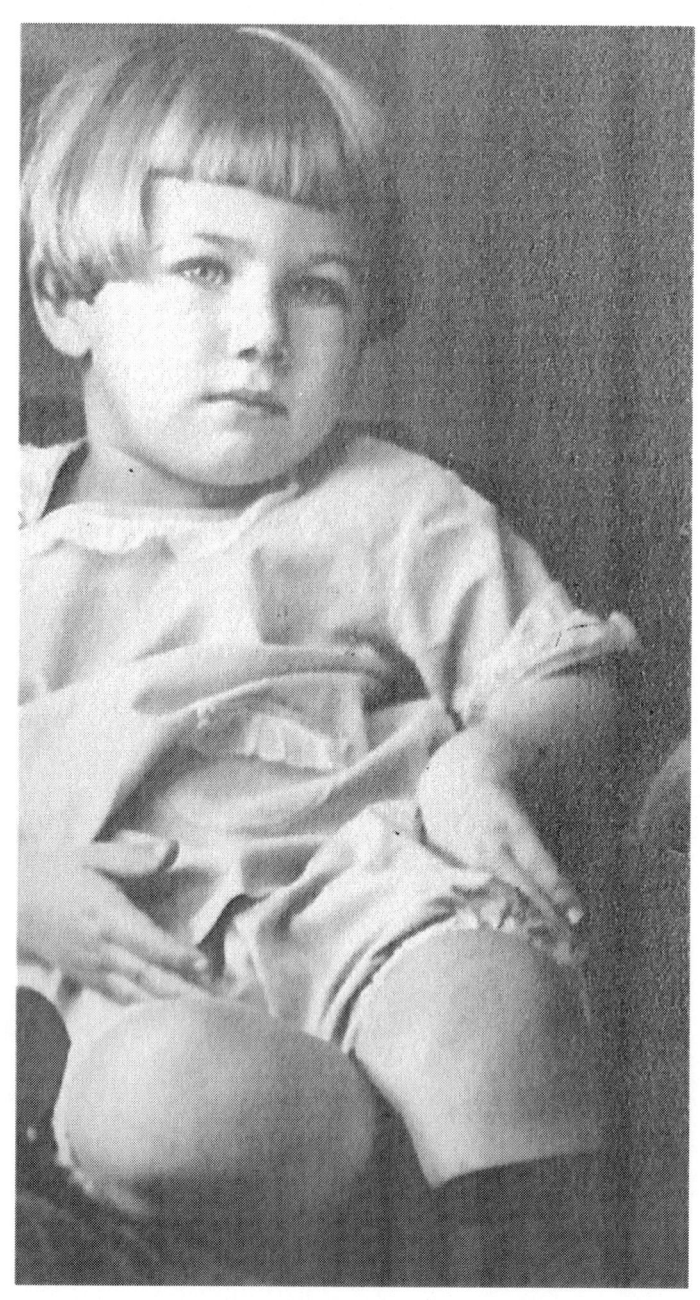

4 years old, 1926

Childhood

"The blessedness of being little!!!"
~ William Shakespeare

    Memories in Melody... just how far back do the memories go? Every story has a beginning and I got to thinking recently about when my love affair with music and records really began. Clearly, so many influences shape who we are and the paths we choose. However, I think I can trace the very beginning to an actual moment.

    I remember a day back in the early 1930's, when I was just ten years old, visiting my grandmother's home in Brooklyn, New York. After wandering around the house and being curious, as ten year old boys are, I came upon my grandmother's hall closet where I found a collection of some old 78rpm records. I was intrigued right away and I asked her if I could play them on the old Victrola.

    I was immediately overwhelmed by the sound and the beauty of the music. I remember a few of my favorites were: "Where Have You Been," "Chloe" and "I'll Always Be In Love With You." I remember the song "Fox Trot." Seeing the title, I wondered at first, if I would hear the sounds of a fox running through the woods! What was a little kid to think?

When I returned to my home in Flatbush where my brother Larry and I shared a third floor bedroom in a rambling old wooden frame home on Glenwood Road. The house had originally been the home of silent screen star, John Bunny. My prized possession suddenly became the family's upright Victrola phonograph. It was not electric and had to be wound regularly. After my experience at my grandparents' home, it became a marvelous machine where I played my growing collection of treasured 78 records with a quality somewhat less than high fidelity. (Who even knew the term at that time.) Most of the records I played were by people like Bing Crosby, Russ Columbo and Dick Powell. Sitting on the floor as a kid in my room in Brooklyn, I never knew that I would one day be able to meet and be associated with these great stars.

By 1937, I included selections by Tommy Dorsey and Benny Goodman. A Dorsey favorite was "The Music Goes Round and Round" and Tommy Dorsey had another hit with "The Dipsy Doodle." These were also the records that we danced to at the Saturday evening Hi-Y dances at the Flatbush YMCA. It was there that I learned to do "The Big Apple" and a mixture of other currently popular dances as "The Shag," "Truckin'," "The Suzy Q" and the "Lindy Hop."

We also danced to the exciting new Benny Goodman Swing Band. Today, the Lindy is only performed by some of the more energetic senior citizens who attend wedding receptions or at events where the band stops rocking to play "In The Mood" or other Big Band Era favorites.

I purchased most of my 78 rpm records in Namm's Basement or on Flatbush Avenue at Amrose Record Shop or Halperin's near Church Avenue. As I got older, it occurred to me that people other than myself might like to hear some of my records. One afternoon I moved the Victrola over to the big bay window which opened out to the street. Using the special steel needles that were labeled "full tone loud," I began playing some of my favorite 78's. I won't say that the neighborhood was overjoyed at the concerts but an occasional passerby would look up and smile.

I also owned a portable wind-up record player which my pals and I took to Riis Park one Saturday. Priorities changed as I became a teenager and the idea was to attract girls to our beach blanket. The music was drowned out by the surf and the people having fun, so all we attracted was sand in the record player. Well, it seemed like a good idea at the time.

About this time, my dad introduced me to the great music of Kern, Berlin, Romberg, Rodgers and the other famous composers of show tunes and movie music. I am still delighted by his Victor Red Seal album of gems from Jerome Kern operettas.

I also learned to enjoy the lilting Strauss waltzes and, thanks to my granddad, a proud member of the 23rd Regiment, I thrilled to the marvelous Sousa marches.

As we moved into the late thirties and early forties, the big bands of Artie Shaw, Count Basie, Duke Ellington and especially Glenn Miller produced many recordings which added to my ever-growing collection. I learned to enjoy other singers besides Bing and Sinatra. I also liked Dick Haymes, Nat Cole and Buddy Clark. Girl singer favorites were and still are, Ella Fitzgerald, Sarah Vaughan, Martha Tilton, Carmen McRae, Teddi King and Rosie Clooney.

Somebody once said "It's all right to look back, just don't stare." It's hard for me not to stare when I recall the days of my youth in dear old Flatbush. I have so many memories, some joyful, some tinged with sadness, but most of my recollections are happy ones. I remember graduating from P.S. 217 on the corner of Newkirk and Coney Island Avenues. The year was 1936. I was just 14. I had my first crush on a little blonde girl in my class named Helen Bowen. My best pal at the time was Walter "Willie" Williams.

The Brooklyn Dodgers were managed by Casey Stengel, the

only man in major league history to manage three New York teams. My dad was a reporter for The Brooklyn Eagle and he had a season pass to Ebbets Field so I got to see many games. In those days, the Dodgers were usually in last place, but I still loved to watch them play. Some of my favorite players were Dolph Camilli, Johnny Cooney, Joe Stripp, Lonnie Frey, Ernie Koy and Van Lingle Mungo. For me, Major League baseball was much more enjoyable in those days. There were only eight teams in each league, no excessive post season or inter-league games, no wild card games or other devices to milk the fans. There were no "cry baby" player strikes, salaries were not astronomical and trades were at a minimum. Pitchers had to take their turn at the plate and we didn't need designated hitters.

Movies in the 30's were not (sorry for the cliché) all murder and mayhem. Car crashes and other violent scenes were rare. Men and women were never seen in bed together and four letter words were virtually unheard of. One of my favorite movies in the 30's was "Follow The Fleet" with Fred Astaire and Ginger Rogers. Remember that beautiful sequence where they danced to Irving Berlin's "Let's Face The Music and Dance"? I also saw "Follow The Fleet" at the RKO Kenmore at Church and Flatbush Avenues across the street from the Old Dutch Reformed Church. My first visits to the movies introduced me to more songs. I loved "The Pagan Love Song" from a Ramon Novarro film "The Pagan." With my uncle Jack at the Babylon Theatre I saw an early Maurice Chevalier picture "Innocents of Paris." It was in that picture that Chevalier sang "Louise" and the song has always been a favorite.

In the early thirties, Bing Crosby appeared in some Mack Sennett short films. His singing intrigued me and oh how I loved those songs, "I Surrender Dear," "Just One More Chance," "Dream House" and "Snuggled On Your Shoulder." Bing was my favorite singer and movie star and has remained so throughout my life. Russ Columbo, another favorite, was a crooner who sadly, died very young. He made a number of memorable recordings, "Prisoner of Love," "You Call It Madness" and "Time On My Hands."

Next I was captivated by the voice and personality of Dick Powell. Two of my early Powell films were "Happiness Ahead" and "Shipmates Forever." I collected all of his records and still enjoy them today. Happily, many of Dick's best songs have been re-released. Other singers I liked growing up in the early and mid-thirties include Ruth Etting, Alice Faye and Ginger Rogers. Ginger wasn't a great singer but displayed a lot of personality.

    My favorite action film was "Lives of a Bengal Lancer" with Gary Cooper and Franchot Tone. I saw that one six times. I also loved "Wake Up and Live" with Alice Faye and Jack Haley. Another favorite was hearing the voice of Buddy Clark on the soundtrack as "The Phantom Troubadour." At the Flatbush theater on Church Avenue, I remember seeing a great stage show with the Will Bradley-Ray McKinley Orchestra. Their big hit was "Beat Me Daddy Eight to The Bar."

    It is agreed upon by many that the era during my entire childhood was one of the greatest in history. The music of the 1930's and 1940's was some of the most beautiful music ever written. The films in those two decades are still considered to be some of the greatest movies ever created. How blessed I am to have grown up during that time. Not only do I always cherish the many wonderful memories with my sister, Ruth, brother, Larry, my parents and grandparents but my time spent listening to music and watching great movies surely shaped me and helped influence my direction. I often valued being alone while listening to all of that great music but in retrospect, when I used to push that old victrola over to the window so passersby could hear, it was also a very clear beginning of my wanting to share my favorite music with the world.

Top: With my mother, Dorothy 1926,
Middle row: At our family home in Brooklyn, in 1937
With my sister Ruth in 1935, with family dog, Freckles, 1937
Bottom row: With my dad, Howard - mid 1940's

With my sister Ruth, 1941

BROOKLYN DAILY EAGLE
NEW YORK CITY, MONDAY, JANUARY 26, 1931.

Stories of Old Brooklyn

Shiebler Built Home Near Park as Hobby

The George W. Shiebler mansion, that was a landmark for many years on Plaza St. near the main entrance to Prospect Park.

Thousands Admired Mansion as Symbol of Old Brooklyn Until Its Destruction to Make Room for Towering Apartment

My great- grandfather's home until it was taken down in 1931. It was one of many casualties due to rebuilding, a lost piece of history and craftsmanship, like too many other great places in New York during the early-mid 1900's.

New York, As It Was

"It couldn't have happened anywhere but in little old New York." ~ O. Henry

I have many fond memories of old New York and particularly Flatbush where I was born and brought up. There I attended grade school, P.S. 139, and P.S. 217 and learned ballroom dancing at Miss Adelaide Molter's School.

However, friends who have recently returned tell me, "Don't go back." One old friend attended a 50th anniversary reunion at Brooklyn Tech High School. He said, "The old neighborhood has sadly changed for the worst, I'm sorry I went back."

In the many years since I last visited New York City, I do continue to hear glowing reports about the improvements in many other areas. The new look in Times Square, the improvements on 42nd Street, the new Ford Center, the skating rink at the South Street Seaport and much more.

In his book, "Heart of the World" (Alfred A. Knopf) Nik Cohn observes, "Times Square has always changed every twenty years, but this time it has changed into a corporate, generic American city that doesn't particularly express the uniqueness of New York."

New York celebrated its 100th birthday in 1998 since being designated as greater New York in 1898. Although in recent years, many good things have been happening and even despite the terrible tragedy of 9/11, New Yorkers banded together and showed their love for their great city and for each other. But something has changed. There was once a distinct feeling about Manhattan, especially for me and for so many of my contemporaries. There was a special charm, especially in the thirties and forties... a charm that no longer exists.

In my youth, New York City was such a great place to visit. Now, much of the "uniqueness" referred to by Mr. Cohn is no longer there. I think sadly of all the famous locations, including many landmarks which have now disappeared. No longer to be found are the following mid-town theaters, The Paramount, Capitol, Strand, Lowe's State, Rivoli, Roxy, Palace, Centre Theatre, Astor, Rialto, Gaiety, The Trans-Lux Newsreel Theatres and others.

I miss the wonderful automat where four nickels bought a delicious beef pie. There were many other inexpensive, tasty dishes. I often wonder if anyone remembers Nedick's orange juice stands and Chock Full 'O Nuts counters? Their specialty was cream cheese sandwiches on date nut bread. My favorites were their sugared, whole wheat doughnuts with a cup of freshly brewed coffee. How about Lindy's cheesecake and McGinnis' roast beef sandwiches? Just around the corner and across the street was Hansen's Drug Store which was a favorite meeting place for show biz folk. There was also Child's Restaurant which offered a meal of chicken croquettes with gravy, mashed potatoes and a roll for 39 cents.

Flagg Brothers sold men's shoes for $4.44 and a nickel would take you anywhere in the subway, on a bus or on the ferry to Staten Island. Before noon, 25 cents would get you into the New York Paramount for a new movie and a great stage show featuring top flight talent. The cover charge in hotel dining rooms for dancing to a name band was only a dollar.

It's true that there are several new and splendid hotels but I will always miss the Grand Old Hotel Astor. The front steps were a favorite meeting place and a great spot to watch the crowds go by. I also miss the New Yorker, The Savoy, The Taft, Dewitt Clinton, McAlpin, Victoria, The Biltmore, The Commodore, The Lincoln, The Vanderbilt, The Piccadilly and The Dixie.

As of 2012, still going strong are the Waldorf Astoria, The Essex House, Ritz Carlton, Sherry- Netherland, The Roosevelt, Algonquin, The Pierre, The Edison and The Pennsylvania which still has part of that famous phone number, Pennsylvania 6-5000. (In 1940, a single room there was only $4.00!)

In downtown Brooklyn, The Hotel St. George and the Bossert have vanished. Loeser's, A & S and Namm's Department Stores are long gone. So is the Brooklyn Paramount, The Fox, Roseland, Minsky's, The Star, The RKO Albee and The Metropolitan. Missing is the Wiliamsburgh Savings Bank, The YMCA, and The Brooklyn Academy which I attended in the same class with actor, Carroll O'Connor.

I wonder if anyone remembers when the Brooklyn Dodgers had their business offices on Montague Street? I also know people who will never forget Joe's Restaurant and Oetjens on Church Avenue in Flatbush.

Flatbush Avenue is remembered for Erasmus Hall High School which I attended. I also recall the beautiful Dutch Reformed Church which I am assured still stands on the corner of Flatbush and Church Avenues. I'm sure I am not the only one who misses the RKO Kenmore, The Patio, Midwood, Leader, Farragut, Beverly and Flatbush Theatres, The Flatbush YMCA, Halperins, and Amrose Record Shops. What fond memories many have of Bickfords and Garfield's Cafeterias, Schraffts, Jahn's Soda Fountain. Trebel's Florist Shops, riding trolley cars. It's painful even to think of Ebbet's Field. I am told that on the site now stands the Jackie Robinson Apartments. A brass plaque on one building shows an arrow indicating where home plate used to be. Ironically, adjacent to that commemoration is another sign that says, "No Ball Playing Allowed."

I suppose it's best to just recall the good times and places. For those of us who lived in those special times, we can close our eyes and visualize the New York we all remember and be thankful we were alive to experience it. If you listen closely, you might hear the thrilling sound of the Benny Goodman Band Playing "Let's Dance" on that rising stage, even Glenn Miller's "Moonlight Serenade" or "Tommy Dorsey's "Getting Sentimental Over You."

The era of the 1930's and 1940's, all who lived through it agree. It seemed like a dream, even while it was happening.

Top left: Working as a Marine combat Correspondent
Top right: Visiting my home in Amityville in uniform
Bottom: With my M1 rifle at Parris Island

The Marines

"It is sweet to serve one's country by deeds, and it is not absurd to serve her by words."   ~Sallust

After I graduated from Brooklyn Academy in 1940, I decided to hold off on college and look into working for a while. My father had been employed for the New York Board of Education in Public Relations and was a respected and brilliant writer. I was always interested in what he did. I knew I needed to work and I was fortunate enough to get a part time job with a public relations firm in Manhattan. My responsibilities included writing press releases and while I didn't know it at the time, this was a skill I would soon need.

In the fall of 1942, I decided to enlist in the Marines. It wasn't a hasty decision as I had always admired that particular branch of the service. I went into Manhattan to the recruiting office at 299 Broadway, was accepted and was sent to Parris Island in South Carolina for boot camp. As anyone can tell you who's been there, Parris Island is certainly not a fun place to be. It's known as a place where "the sand is fourteen inches deep and the sun is scorching hot." However, I tried to put the daunting challenge in perspective and I reminded myself that I could do anything for ten weeks.

The training was rigorous and it was also ultimately good for me as I got into shape. Aside from developing my stamina, like many other fellow marines, I worked hard at becoming an accomplished sharpshooter. Once, when I was shooting at the rifle range, I was doing brilliantly until a fog rolled in at the 500 yard distance. I couldn't see the targets well enough but was told that I would have received the distinction of "expert" had I been able to finish with the same consistent precision I had shown. I was honored to achieve the second highest rating in my platoon and I received a sharp shooter medal, which has since been passed down to my granddaughter Christa upon her request.

When I was finished boot camp in the winter of 1943, I was transferred to Pearl Harbor. Because of a mild heart condition and with recognition of my public relations experience, I applied and was assigned to the duties of Marine Combat Correspondent. As our soldiers returned from combat, I interviewed them and wrote about each of their personal stories. The stories in turn were published in their hometown newspapers.

After a year, I was transferred to Marine headquarters in New York City under Captain Norman White. I continued my work as a combat correspondent and started visiting injured soldiers in hospitals. I was eager to share their stories with the rest of the country. I worked in New York for about two years. In my leisure time, I went to see the latest film or my greatest thrill, going to the Paramount to see Dick Powell or Benny Goodman.

Before World War II ended in 1945, my last year as a correspondent was spent in Washington D.C. and my byline was "Sgt. Ellsworth Shiebler." Washington would be the place where I would first meet Bing Crosby and a place where I would ultimately be relieved to be working. While in D.C, it was quite disconcerting to learn that the office I had worked in while in New York was hit by a B-25 Mitchell bomber which crashed in the fog while on a routine personal transport mission from Boston to New York. The plane hit in the vicinity of the building where my office had been for two years. Tragically, fourteen people were killed that day. Along with the great loss of life during over four years of combat, our war weary nation was relieved when it was finally over that same year.

I was extremely proud to be a Marine and I still am to this day. It was obviously a great outfit. I met many brave soldiers, many whose stories I will never forget. I hope through my writing that many of those articles gave insight to the plight and sacrifice of our service men and women. It was an important time in my life, one of not only discipline but of preparation for a career that I had never dreamed was about to become a reality.

While I was stationed in Pearl Harbor, Hawaii, pointing to my home state of New York! 1943

While in Pearl Harbor, Hawaii, a photo with my buddies, Hal Goodwin, and David Stephenson, 1943

Above: Ovetta Culp Hobby of American National Red Cross issues proclamation pledging added support to all branches of the service September 1943. (I am third from the left in the back row) Photo credit: Harris & Ewing

While in the Marines, I was called to do a photo session acting as a wounded Marine veteran on behalf of the Ethyl Corporation.

War-Time Hawaiian Islands Pictured by Shiebler

Marine Corps Combat Correspondent Says Glamour Is Gone; Services Have Taken Over

Sgt. Ellsworth A. Shiebler, Combat Correspondent for the Marine Corps wrote the following story describing the war-time Hawaiian Islands. Sgt. Shiebler is the son of Mr. and Mrs. Howard A. Shiebler of Amityville.

Somewhere in the Hawaiian Islands — (Delayed) — "The mere mention of Hawaii brings to mind thoughts of pineapples, grass skirts, and singing guitars. Parents, sweethearts, and friends of servicemen in Hawaii undoubtedly wonder if the place is as glamorous as Hollywood has it cracked up to be. The Hawaiian Chamber of Commerce may object, but the answer is a big "NO."

Before the war, tourists were Hawaii's third largest industry. Steamship lines' pamphlets raved on about this Pacific paradise, with the glistening white sands and inviting surf at Waikiki, the lavish Royal Hawaiian Hotel, majestic mountains capped with fleecy clouds, the quaint, picturesque shops in Honolulu, and extensive sugar cane fields and pineapple plantations covering many thousands of acres.

Today the "tourists" either wear khaki, navy blue, or the dungarees of a war worker. Obviously they are not here to relax in the shade of a swaying palm, but when they do have a few leisure hours, they more often than not expect too much in the way of so-called "glamor."

One of the first things that soldier, sailor, or Marine will do is look for a grass skirt to send home to his girl friend. He soon learns that he'd have a better chance of seeing such scant attire on Betty Grable doing a hula dance before the cameras on a Southern California movie lot.

Sure, you can pick up a grass skirt in a souvenir shop, but don't be surprised if you find a tag attached which reads, "Brooklyn, New York." Grass skirts made in Hawaii are as rare as chop suey in China.

Honolulu is the largest city in area in the whole world and transportation facilities are much the same as in any large city in the United States today.

Unfortunately the bus driver's inevitable plea of "Kindly move to the rear" meets with the same response as it does in crowded buses on New York City's Fifth ave., or on Pennsylvania ave., in Washington, D. C.

There is one big difference, however. Native Islanders, particularly the younger set, often omit shoes from their regular daily wearing apparel. The difficulty among standees on public vehicles is therefore obvious... ("Ouch! my corns!")

The serviceman is usually quite amazed by the interesting contrasts of the South Seas, Orient, and the Occident. He learns that the islands offer sports of all kinds, from skiing on the snowy slopes of Mauna Kea to surfboard polo at Waikiki Beach.

As far as oddities are concerned, here are a few:—President Franklin D. Roosevelt is the only United States President to visit Hawaii... billboards are not permitted... there are no snakes on the islands... sugar cane fields are set on fire to destroy trash before harvesting, and it takes about 18 months for one harvest... on Christmas Day, Santa

(Continued on Page Eight)

Excerpt from one of the many articles I wrote as a combat correspondent

Top: At my home in Amityville NY aboard our family boat the "Marion"

Bottom: With my good friend, singer Dick Powell, in 1942

Part II

The Next Fifty Years

Just before entering radio full- time, I did a brief modeling stint in New York

Reading a commercial on T.V. in New York

Typing a music sheet for my show.

Live on the air!... at WHIM with a Benny Goodman record set in the foreground.

Visiting with the proprietors of a local record shop in Providence. (Notice the old radios in the background!)

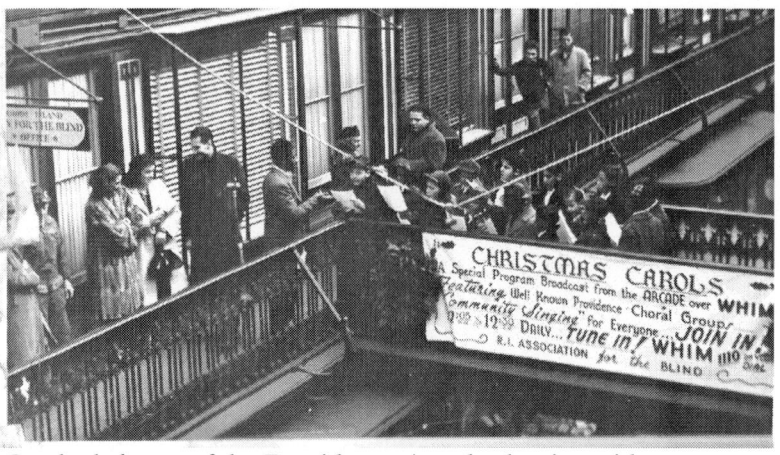

On the balcony of the Providence Arcade chatting with two listeners while broadcasting a show which featured local choral groups during the Christmas season.

Providence

"If there is anything that a man can do well, I say let him do it. Give him a chance."   ~Abraham Lincoln

After the war ended, I worked in New York City for the U.S.O. for about six months. I then decided to go to college and applied to Brown University in Providence, Rhode Island and was accepted. I was fortunate enough to be able to go on the G.I. Bill of Rights. I decided to study journalism and started familiarizing myself with Providence and the surrounding area.

During my first few weeks in town, I began hearing about a local radio station called WHIM which was very popular and rated number one in Providence. I began to listen and was amazed at how similar their format was to my own musical tastes. It was all of the music and artists I had always enjoyed and it was also very similar to WNEW in New York.

While listening to the station, the music, and the announcers, I began to think about how much I would enjoy being a disc jockey there. There were no openings in the Want Ads, no job offers in the local papers but I wondered if I could just go to the station and apply. My only experience in radio was when Bronx Disc Jockey Art Ford invited me in the early 40's to be a guest on his show on WBNX. I brought along some of my best Bing Crosby records and did have a few words on the air. It was quite a thrill. Also, as a freshman at Brown, I had a little show on WBRU, a key station of the intercollegiate broadcasting system which could only be heard on campus. I remember the first record I played was Tommy Dorsey's "This Is The Beginning of The End" featuring Frank Sinatra. However, to apply to a well known and respected station like WHIM, I lacked the real experience a DJ would need. My confidence was based solely on my extensive record collection, my knowledge of the artists and perhaps even the memory of myself as a young boy, pretending to be a famous disc jockey named "Tommy Connors" who created his own radio show every day while walking home from school.

While considering the idea of auditioning, I started to think that perhaps my given name, "Ellsworth Shiebler" was, at best, not very easy to pronounce correctly and, at worst, hardly a DJ sounding name. I thought of a few ideas and then had a thought of my Uncle Jack of whom I had always been quite fond. I tried out the sound of his name paired with my first name as a last name. "Jack Ellsworth" instantly sounded right to me! Armed with no professional radio experience, some public relations experience and a new name, I hoped that I had the talent to present it all on the air. There was only one way to find out.

I showed up at the WHIM studio one day with my record collection and respectfully asked to see the manager. Surprisingly, they interviewed me and let me audition by reading a newscast. When I was finished, one of the managers came running into the studio. Bob Engles said to his partner, George Taylor, "Where'd you get this kid?... He hasn't got it!" George replied, speaking in my direction, "You're just what we're looking for!" After the initial criticism from Bob Engles, I immediately looked around the studio to see if George was addressing someone other than me.

I said, "Mr Taylor are you talking to me?" "Yes!!" he enthusiastically replied. He turned to to Bob and said, "Believe me, he's got the stuff!" I was hired on the spot.

    I enjoyed doing my newly assigned shows more than I had imagined. I had the opportunity to do personal appearances. I met so many new people and learned so much about radio and the business in general. Within weeks, the fan mail starting pouring in. Bob Engles later admitted to George Taylor that he had initially been wrong about me and he was very glad that I was hired. This was truly the start of something that I felt was my proverbial "calling." It was that moment many people have in life when you know what you were born to do.

    To this day I consider George Taylor one of the "pivotal people" in my life. Here was a man who knew nothing about me, who knew I had no experience but he saw my enthusiasm, he saw me give all I had. While it sounds like a cliché, he genuinely believed in me. That one act of faith set a course for my entire future and I have been grateful every day since.

    I stayed at WHIM from 1946-1948, went over to WFCI for a while and even did a stint at WVNJ in Newark, New Jersey. However, I will always have the fondest memories of my start in radio at WHIM in Providence. It's amazing when I think of what George Taylor did that first day taking the time to give me a chance. It should make us realize how much of a difference we all can make in someone's life. You hear it time and time again, in sports, in music, in apprenticeship programs, even in family relationships that the act of helping someone to follow a goal is so important. All most of us need when we are young, is to have just one person who takes the time, just one caring individual who has the faith to help us dare to do what we could never attempt alone.

Thank you George Taylor, from Jack Ellsworth.
Thank you as well Mr. Taylor, from that "famous" eleven year old DJ named "Tommy Connors," doing his radio show every day walking home from school, who never dreamed that he'd really get the chance.

(top): In the Studio in Providence
(bottom): Broadcasting Live from the window of a local record store

Wherever records are sold, you're apt to run into Jack. An enthusiastic collector, his assemblage includes everything that Bing Crosby ever put on a platter as well as classics by Columbo, Sinatra and Goodman.

Jack originates many of his record shows outside our studios — at "Y" canteens and at several young people's clubs. In addition, he has put on special shows at Hope and Cranston High Schools as well as many local clubs.

The Y.M.C.A. East Side Division on Summit Avenue will open its canteen doors tomorrow night for members of senior high schools. A canteen for junior high students will open tonight. A guest will be welcomed by the senior high gals and boys on Saturday eve, he's that handsome disc-jockey from WHIM, Jack Ellsworth.

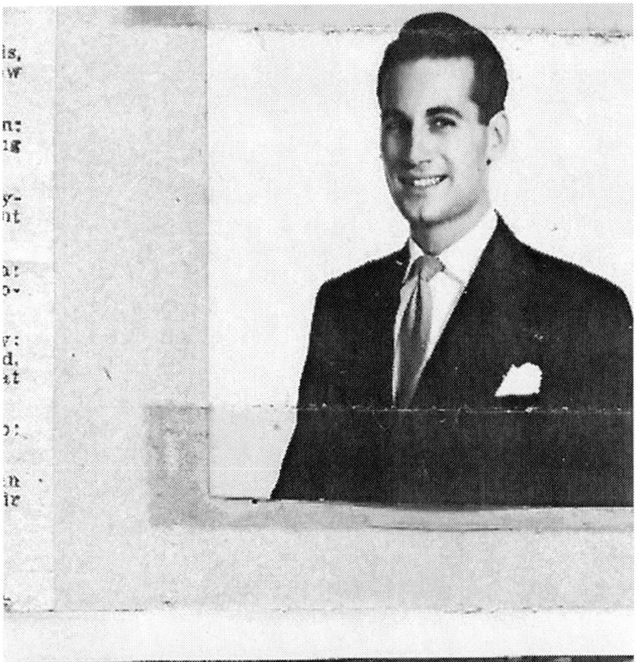

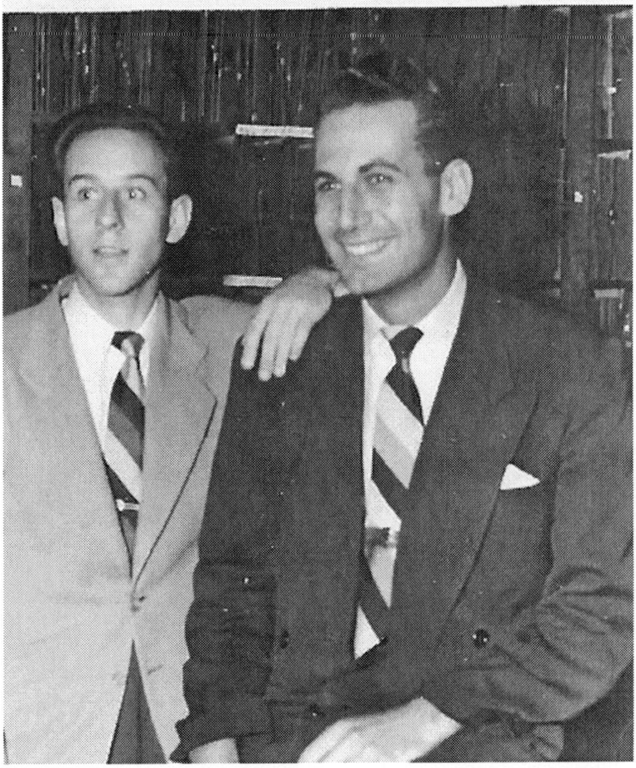

PROVIDENCE, R. I., OCTOBER 31, 1947

Surrounding Jack Ellsworth at the stage door are l. to r.: Gerhardt, Apkarian, Colonna Silvestri, Temkin, Irving Silverman, Janice Swanson, Norma Reid, Winifred Barber and Melvin Shuman.

Variety 1947

Jack Ellsworth

WHIM'S disc jockey, Jack Ellsworth, has a dynamic personality that is transmitted in his voice. Jack has a good line, but above all possesses a natural sense of what people like in music. He was initiated into radio by assisting Art Ford on "The Milkman's Matinee" in New York.

It was because of his extensive collection of words and his ability to put them over, that he received his introduction to WHIM. He is fast developing a technique that will put him into the "Martin Block" class.

Ellsworth is only 25 and still attends a local college on a part-time basis. His favorite bands, as his audiences know, are Tommy Dorsey, Glenn Miller, and Benny Goodman. In the singing line he prefers Bing Crosby, Frank Sinatra, Dick Haymes, Martha Tilton, Margaret Whiting and Byrl Davis.

Many of the younger set who frequent canteens and high school clubs have seen him originate his shows from their local spots.

You Ought to Know
JACK ELLSWORTH

Jack is a disc-jockey who has done some thinking about his job.
"Too many disc-jockeys today are on the wrong kick," Jack feels. "A jockey's primary function is to play records, read commercials, and make occasional intelligent comments on the records and the artists".

He is particularly opposed to "deejays who fancy themselves as comedians, crooners, or who indulge in prolonged telephone conversations on the air."

Many of the records Jack plays on his WFCI show are from his own large library which includes a complete collection by Bing Crosby, Frank Sinatra, Benny Goodman, Tommy Dorsey and Glenn Miller.

Jack is 27 years old, single, and was a former Marine Corp Combat Correspondent.

Newspaper clippings including part of a column from the weekly entertainment magazine, Variety, 1947

Back in Rhode Island!

JACK ELLSWORTH

Jack's vacation, under the doctor's orders, is over. He's yours again with his sparkling "thisa and thata" . . . and the day's latest platter . . .

Afternoons on

WFCI

1420 ON YOUR DIAL

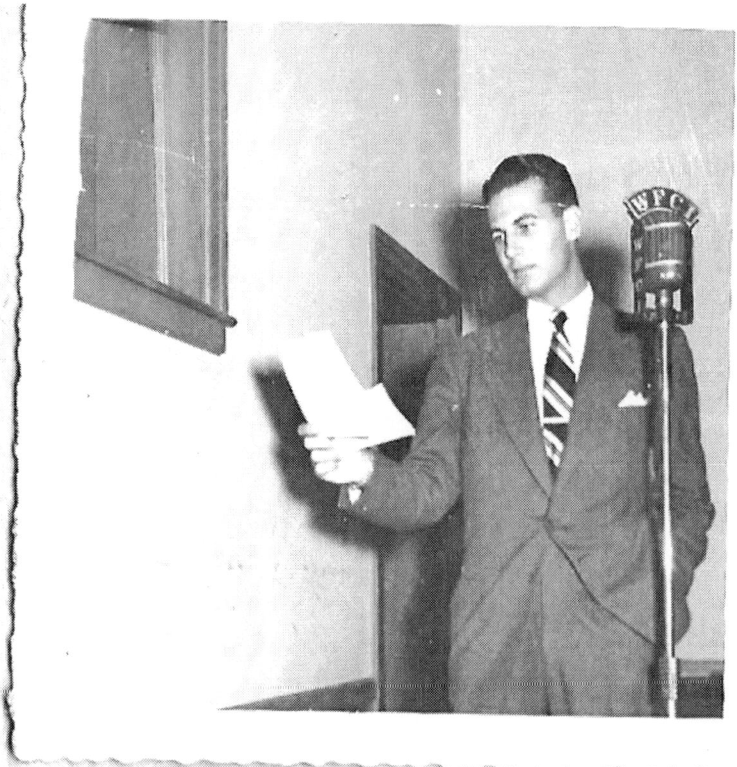

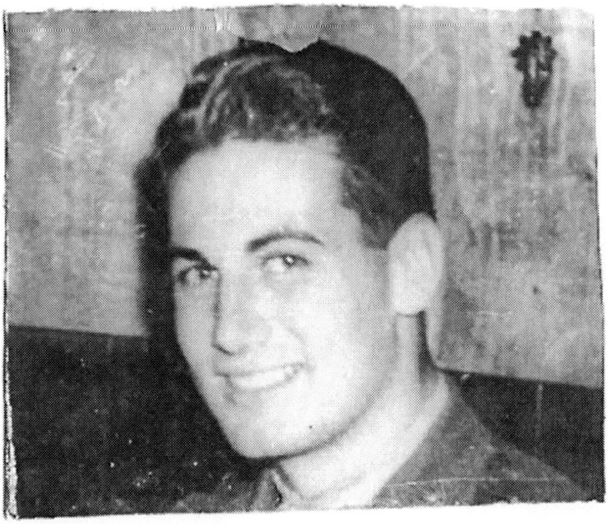

Some amazing artwork (originally done in color) by one of my loyal fans, while I was on hiatus.

the jumping jockeys

jumping jack

rhode island's favorite jockey looks as good as he sounds

LONG ISLAND'S loss is Rhode Island's gain, in the opinion of listeners to WFCI's Jack Ellsworth. The handsome ex-Marine started a post-war radio career at WHIM in Providence while he was attending Brown, and after a vacation from an over-strenuous schedule, returned this spring to the ABC affiliate in that city.

On an early afternoon show, Jack concentrates on old records of standards, on the late afternoon stint he sticks close to jazz, and at 6:45 PM he rounds out his day with fifteen minutes of Glenn Miller, before rushing off to a portable radio to hear his favorite singer, Frank Sinatra, over another network. Whichever show you catch, the catchword is "discriminating." The music Jack plays is strictly for listeners who are anti-corn. "I try never to insult the intelligence of discriminating listeners," he says. "I have no objection to an obviously commercial recording as long as it is musically good." Those who qualify as musically good include Woody, Krupa, Thornhill, Benny, Dizzy, Bird, Shearing, Tristano, Tatum ("what a threesome!") and Lester, plus a wide variety of singers led by Frank. Feature of the jazz show is a series of recorded interviews with everyone from Damone to Herman.

Though he doesn't want to be a disc jockey for the rest of his life, Jack gets a kick out of what he's doing, gives thanks to the station for getting his own conscience be his guide, and enjoys his appreciative fan clubs—"thank heaven there are enough intelligent and hip people to encourage and inspire the jumping jockeys!"—B.H.

two voices

JANUARY, 1950

Article from Metronome Magazine

A sampling of the large volume of fan mail I was so humbled to receive. Providence 1949

Collection of handwritten fan letters to Jack Ellsworth:

Dear Jack,

Your programs are Very Great! I think you are Mr. Radio! Especially enjoyed your memorial to Buddy Clark! Have been listening to you for 2½ yrs. now, and never hear enough!

...picture, and will keep on listening to you, because you are the most wonderful radio announcer we have ever had in Rhode Island! Your interest in trying to please all the listeners (and that is tough) and your kindness to everyone is deeply appreciated.

Thanks, and take care of yourself.

Mary E. Phillips

"You deserve no less for we cannot even start to evaluate the joy and pleasure you passed on to the Providence radio audi—

J. F. - The "Him" in WHIM.

Dotty T.

...sure sounds good to hear them during the day while I'm at work. I think you're doing a terrific job at WHIM, and I'm sure this opinion is shared by thousands here in R. I. We've needed something like WHIM here for years and it's fine to know that we've finally got it.

Dear Jack Ellsworth,

I want to tell you how I enjoy your program. I can see why people call you the best disc jockey in Rhode Island. I hope you keep on doing the good work.

Love the way you conduct guest interviews. Make us...

Dear Jack Ellsworth,

Just a line to let you know how much I enjoy your program. I have been confined to bed for two weeks and the records you play from 10 to 12 really give my morale a boost!

Your delivery is perfect! By the way, has anyone ever told you, you talk like Frank Sinatra?

1949

I enjoy your program very much. Have been stuck in the house almost 2 years. Your program...

53

At the CopaCabana in 1950 honoring vocalist Sarah Vaughan. L-R: Bill Gordon, Sarah Vaughan, George Treadwell, Jack Ellsworth, Bill Kirby, Hal Tunnis, Max Cole and Mitch Miller of Columbia Records.
Photo credit: Popsie

New love.... Autumn of '51

Meeting Dot

"Hear my soul speak. Of the very instant that I saw you, did my heart fly at your service."
~William Shakespeare

In 1950, after working at WVNJ in Newark, New Jersey, I decided to go back to my roots on Long Island. I heard about a radio station on the island called WGSM. They had a great format and were located in Huntington not too far from my home in Amityville. I applied for a job and was fortunate enough to begin working there right away. Even though I had never missed a Thanksgiving or Christmas at home with my family in all those years out of state, it was good to be back on Long Island and I was hoping to stay.

My hopes were about to be realized. In the same building as WGSM, there were a few other offices, including a lawyer's office. One day, I saw a pretty, young legal secretary with dark hair and freckles come out of the lawyer's office. Now, over the years I had the opportunity to meet a lot of girls from Hollywood and even in Providence but none of them really made a lasting impression. Suddenly, I see this cute girl with freckles ... and I immediately also see something more. I started a few conversations with her and quickly asked her to lunch. We saw each other at work every day and when she started bringing me soup for lunch, I was hopeful that she felt the same way that I did about her. Within weeks, I was completely won over, not just by how pretty she was, but by her caring demeanor, her sense of humor and her strong personality. I just knew I was going to marry her, I thought, "This is my girl."

I brought her home to meet my parents and they immediately loved her too. By September, we had only been dating for about a month, when one evening we were sitting on a hammock in her yard in Cold Spring Harbor. I told her that I loved her and that I wanted her to marry me. She said "Yes!' right away and the hammock broke, leaving us on the ground in laughter! She said that she had a sense that I was going to ask her, which in retrospect doesn't surprise me. Since the day we met, Dot has had a "sense" about everything, from raising our children, to cooking, to decorating our home, to understanding me. She has been the person who has helped me write copy and commercials and run our business. To this day, she does all of the billing and still types the music sheets and logs for our show on her electric typewriter. Over the years, everyone who has ever met Dot has a personal story about her compassion for others, about how selfless she is and about her strength of character. She has put up with me for over 60 years, taken care of me when I have had some health setbacks and is now my on air co-host. Of all of the changes and decisions I have made over the years, I tell everyone, marrying Dot was the smartest move I have ever made.

She had to know that marrying me wouldn't be easy. We were married on November 24, 1951. I had recently applied to a new station that was just starting called WALK. As fate would have it, I received the position and was asked to start on November 25th, the day after we were married. We had no honeymoon. We were married with family and friends gathered around and then spent one night at the Patchogue Hotel, now the site of the Tiffany Apartments on Main Street in Patchogue. The next morning, I got up bright and early, asked Dot to find us a place to live and I headed off to my new position at WALK. Having just married an amazing girl who would forever change my life, I likewise was about to start a job which would also change my career for the better.

Our wedding day, November 24th 1951

Our wedding reception, 1951

Enjoying dinner at a favorite restaurant, 1982

At home, Christmas 2010

With Dot, enjoying a special moment before attending a fund raising dinner. This same photo hangs in our home with a special poem I wrote especially for her.

MEET YOUR W-A-L-K RADIO FAVORITES

JACK ELLSWORTH
Program Director WALK

WALK'S program director since the station's inception over ten years ago, Jack Ellsworth, also conducts the popular WALK feature program "Memories in Melody." Musically Jack likes "good moody stuff and swinging big bands with a little Sinatra and Keely Smith tossed in. However," he quickly adds, "at WALK we try to program a wide variety of the best music available, ever-mindful of good taste and high standards." "Just because a record may be a hit in some circles," Jack says, "doesn't mean we will play it. Musical trash has no place on WALK at anytime."

Jack served over two years in the South Pacific as a Marine Corps combat correspondent and began his radio career at Brown University's campus station while a student there on the G. I. bill. From there Jack spent three years as the top deejay in Providence, R. I. A native Long Islander, Jack is a past president of the Patchogue Kiwanis Club and teaches a Sunday School class at the Patchogue Congregational Church. Jack has done considerable TV announcing and acting but says he has never been happier than he is at WALK. "This is the job I have always wanted," he enthuses. "Programming for the growing Long Island radio audience is the most fascinating and challenging job I could ask for."

HEAR JACK WEEKDAY MORNINGS AT TEN

AM-1370 KC   **W-A-L-K**   FM-97.5 MC

Newspaper clipping - WALK

Interviewing Miss America in the 60's

WALK and WLIM

"Destiny is no matter of chance. It is a matter of choice. It is not a thing to be waited for, it is a thing to be achieved." ~ William Jennings Bryan

While their main studios were being built on Colonial Drive In East Patchogue, WALK started in a small office in Patchogue above the Arch Preserver Shoe Store on Main Street. WALK was playing familiar standards and based on my experience at the three previous stations, I was hired as their program director. Among the partners who hired me was the famous news reporter, Chet Huntley and owner Ed Wood who would also become my friend and one of my most important mentors. We worked very hard and soon the programming of "Ballads, Blues and Big Bands too" became a format that everyone was raving about.

Dot and I lived for a while in Bellport, renting houses first across from the golf course and then renting next to the Methodist Church. After the birth of our first son, Gary in 1954, (inspired by

Bing Crosby's naming of his first son "Gary") we moved to our current home in East Patchogue, where our next son Glenn was born in 1956. Glenn of course was named after none other than orchestra leader Glenn Miller! Our daughter, Susan followed in 1962, named after my dear grandmother. After my father raved about having two sons and a daughter, we were also thrilled to add a little girl to our family.

In 1965, I was promoted to station manager at WALK. In 1975, I became President, General Manager and CEO. In those great years at WALK, I had the honor of meeting and hiring some great announcers that our listeners still remember to this day. People like newscaster, Joe Ripley, announcer, Kurt Russell, Bob Dorian, George Drake and Ken Bell were co-workers and also friends.

In 1966, I also hired Bob Klein, a favorite of many. At first, Bob started doing evenings and overnights (at that time, WALK FM used to go off-the-air at 2 AM). Our morning man Bob Dorian left in the early 70's for TV work and we gave Bob Klein the morning slot from 5:00 to 9:00. His show was called "Klein til Nine." That morning show would one day become the now famous WALK Breakfast Club with Mark and Cindy.

In 1980, WALK was sold. Dot, George Drake and I decided to partner on a new venture and we purchased the WYFA radio station on Woodside Avenue in Medford, N.Y. We decided to use the call letters WLIM, standing for "Long Island Music." I was flattered to see buses around town with posters on the back advertising WLIM with the slogan, "Jack's Back!"

For the next 20 years, we made WLIM our home away from home and we welcomed so many people there who said it also felt like home. Every record was hand-picked from our extensive LP and growing CD library from my 50 year collection. We entertained celebrities like Benny Goodman and Jerry Vale. We had our every day listeners stop in for visits and we would ask them to stay for lunch. Our son Glenn worked with us in sales and met his lovely wife Marilyn, one of our newscasters. Many of our listeners loved meeting our wonderful secretaries, Patti and Elaine and stopped in to chat with Bob Stern, who brilliantly hosted our Broadway Hollywood Show.

We brought our two golden retrievers to work with us every day. We had our little grandson Michael when he was only five, help read the weather and charm our listeners with his endearing Christmas messages. We hosted community minded events and annual toy drives for Little Flower Children's Services. On the air, we helped find lost pets, we announced school closings and we played specific songs that our listeners requested. If someone called looking for a special, long lost song, we would try to find it and even mail it to them on a cassette. If a business or company advertised with us, we had them come in and do an on air interview at no charge. We always gave personal endorsements for each of our sponsors.

In 2001, I had just turned 79 and we decided to assume fewer responsibilities. I had no plans of actually retiring and we definitely wanted to keep the great music alive for our listeners but we knew that running a full time business was becoming a little difficult to manage at our age! We all agreed that it was time to sell WLIM. It was a bittersweet decision and we still wanted to work but needed to somehow find a happy medium.

One day, amazingly, we happened to speak to someone at WALK and they said they would love to have me back to do my show every weekday including my show "Sundays with Sinatra." After selling WLIM, we came back to WALK and were so touched by how warmly we were received and have been ever since! It seemed almost like destiny to come back to where it all started.

Dot has since joined me on the air and it's where we are three days a week to this very day. My daughter Susan works with us and our granddaughter Elissa even helps me program some of the selections for the show as she is especially fond of the music that I love. Our grandson Matthew, now 17, is our board operator and reports the weather on every show. He helps us with anything and everything that is technical in the studio! At 90 years of age, I have evolved with the radio industry from 78's to LP's to CD's but I need a little assistance with the digital age so I can focus on bringing the great music to our devoted listeners! I have no plans to retire and as long as the good Lord allows, I will keep playing the music of the "Golden Era," ever so grateful to the faithful listeners who have stayed with us all of these years.

Come to Jack Ellsworth's Grand Union Shopper Party Every Saturday 10 A.M. to 11 A.M.

Over W.A.L.K.
Completely Live broadcast from the Patchogue Grand Union.

★ Games ★
★ Prizes ★
★ Surprises ★

Come on over & join the fun & excitement at Grand Union of Patchogue.

1966-67

Newspaper clippings, ads, WALK

MEET YOUR W-A-L-K RADIO FAVORITES

Jack Ellsworth

Ex-Marine Jack Ellsworth was Flatbush born but has lived in Suffolk most of his life. Jack has been in radio since the late forties when he began his radio career in Providence, while still a Brown University Student. A past president and still active member of the Patchogue Kiwanis Club, Jack also teaches a Sunday School class at the Patchogue Congregational Church. Father of two, with another one "on the way," Jack proudly proclaims his boys are natural born ball players. (Look out Mantle and Maris!) Musically, Jack goes for the big band sounds, tasteful vocals a la Sinatra, Doris Day and Ray Conniff. Says he feels sorry for the kids of today who missed the "Golden Era of Dance Bands."

YOU CAN RELIVE THOSE YEARS ON JACK'S DAILY 10 A.M. RECORD SHOW, "MEMORIES IN MELODY," WHICH IS NOW IN ITS TENTH YEAR ON W-A-L-K

AM-1370 KC   **W-A-L-K**   FM-97.5 MC

Children's Corner .... GR 5-8283

RADIO STATION WALK'S BEST FANS are Glenn, 10; Susan, 4, and Gary, 12, Shiebler, the children of Mr. and Mrs. Ellsworth A. Shiebler of East Patchogue. Their dad is known professionally as Jack Ellsworth, station manager of WALK.

A newspaper clipping about my beautiful children, Gary, Glenn and Susan

THURSDAY, JANUARY 7, 1965

Jack Ellsworth Becomes WALK's Station Manager

PROMOTED to station manager of WALK is Jack Ellsworth, program director since the station's inception. He is a resident of East Patchogue.

Jack Ellsworth, WALK's program director since the station's inception, has been elevated to the position of station manager, it was announced this week by Edward W. Wood, Jr., president of Island Broadcasting System.

Mr. Wood pointed out that this promotion, besides being well-deserved, is part of Island Broadcasting's long-range management planning involved in various communications expansion moves in Suffolk County. The most recent of these was its December 1964 application for UHF television Channel 75, presently allocated to the Patchogue area.

Mr. Ellsworth, a long-time resident of the Patchogue area, began his radio career at the Brown University Station after serving with the U.S. Marine Corps in the South Pacific.

A native Long Islander, he is a past president of the Patchogue Kiwanis Club, a director of the Patchogue Chamber of Commerce, a Sunday School teacher in the Congregational Church of Patchogue, and a willing and ready volunteer to such civic activities as the YMCA and Brookhaven Memorial Hospital.

Interviewing Chet Huntley, 1965

MEET YOUR W-A-L-K RADIO FAVORITES

JACK ELLSWORTH
Program Director WALK

WALK'S program director since the station's inception over ten years ago, Jack Ellsworth, also conducts the popular WALK feature program "Memories in Melody." Musically Jack likes "good moody stuff and swinging big bands with a little Sinatra and Keely Smith tossed in. However," he quickly adds, "at WALK we try to program a wide variety of the best music available, ever-mindful of good taste and high standards." "Just because a record may be a hit in some circles," Jack says, "doesn't mean we will play it. Musical trash has no place on WALK at anytime."

Jack served over two years in the South Pacific as a Marine Corps combat correspondent and began his radio career at Brown University's campus station while a student there on the G. I. bill. From there Jack spent three years as the top deejay in Providence, R. I. A native Long Islander, Jack is a past president of the Patchogue Kiwanis Club and teaches a Sunday School class at the Patchogue Congregational Church. Jack has done considerable TV announcing and acting but says he has never been happier than he is at WALK. "This is the job I have always wanted," he enthuses. "Programming for the growing Long Island radio audience is the most fascinating and challenging job I could ask for."

HEAR JACK WEEKDAY MORNINGS AT TEN

AM-1370 KC **W-A-L-K** FM-97.5 MC

Newspaper ad thanking all of my loyal listeners for their support at our new station WLIM

Proclamation

Whereas: the Town of Brookhaven recognizes the efforts of outstanding citizens who have contributed their time, talents and energy to the benefit of our residents; and

Whereas: Jack Ellsworth has been an important part of his community, giving of himself to the residents of Brookhaven through his work in many community organizations including the Executive Board of the Suffolk County Boy Scouts of America, Brookhaven Memorial Hospital's Advisory Board, and the Patchogue Kiwanis Club; and

Whereas: Jack Ellsworth has always shown enthusiasm in finding innovative ways to improve the quality of life for our residents and has been recognized as a "spark" to the business community in the Town of Brookhaven with his dedication as a caring Town resident and member of the Bellport Chamber of Commerce, where he served as President; and

Whereas: Jack's contributions to his community are numerous and duly reflected in the awards that cover his walls at radio station WLIM, where he is CEO and popular radio show host affectionately dubbed "The Silver Fox"; and

Whereas: Jack opens his station to the community to be used as a collection point for holiday food and gift drives for the less fortunate and donates free radio promotional time to charity; and

Whereas: during his 45 years in broadcasting, Jack has devoted himself to his family and his community; and

Whereas: the Town of Brookhaven wishes to pay tribute to Jack Ellsworth for his achievements, his loving spirit and his concern for others.

Now, therefore, I, John LaMura, Supervisor of the Town of Brookhaven, do hereby proclaim October 21, 1992 as

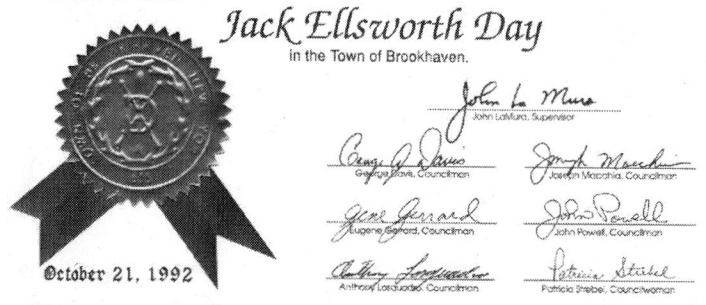

Jack Ellsworth Day
in the Town of Brookhaven.

John LaMura, Supervisor
George Davis, Councilman
Joseph Macchia, Councilman
Eugene Gerrard, Councilman
John Powell, Councilman
Anthony Lasquadro, Councilman
Patricia Strebel, Councilwoman

October 21, 1992

Proclamation I was so honored to receive in 1992.

With Dot and Monsignor Fagan. This was our annual Toy Drive at WLIM for Little Flower Children's Services
Jim Mooney Photo

At WLIM, with, our grandson, Michael, who started making guest appearances on the air to help with the weather when he was just three! He is now almost 22 years old and along with my 17 year old grandson Matthew, they still help with my show on WALK.

Top left: With Dot and her mother, Lillie and baby Gary, 1954
Top right: With my baby nephew, Jeff (on shoulders) Glenn (2) and Gary (4), 1958 2nd row left: With Dot on an outing, early 1960's 2nd row right: Gary, Glenn and Susan pose for a Christmas card, 1965 Bottom left: With Glenn (16) Susan (10) 1972 Bottom right: At home on our porch, 1971

Family and Faith

"A man is not where he lives, but where he loves."
~Latin Proverb

To this day, I greatly enjoy the radio business. It has been an honor to be able to present the talents of so many legendary performers. Radio has been my life for over 65 years. I hope to keep going as long as I can. Retirement is a word I don't know. If I can recall fond memories of these performers for my listeners then I have achieved the purpose of "Memories in Melody."

My career would never have been successful or flourished all these years if it weren't for my supportive and loving wife, Dot. I tell people in the sixty plus years that Dot and I have been married that we have never exchanged a cross word! Of course this is untrue for us or for anyone who is married! Dot and I have exchanged many cross words over the years and many loving words. In the last few years, I have come to learn that even her cross words are in many ways... the same as her loving words. She always has my best interest at heart. Everyone who knows me credits her with keeping me in line. As men, we start to value that assistance as years go by!

Many of my listeners now look forward to hearing Dot as she has joined me on the air in recent years! In addition to Dot's help, our daughter Susan is our personal assistant and helps with sales and social networking. My 19 year old granddaughter Elissa helps me program the selections for the show each week. After years of hearing the great artists, Elissa now loves the music as much as I do! As I bring the music and my knowledge to the microphone, Dot helps write and read the commercials and public service announcements. Our 17 year old grandson Matthew reads the weather while utilizing his technical expertise to run the board. Our older grandson Michael, who is now 21, also "co-hosts" the show with me from time to time. So many of our listeners remember Michael from his days as a young boy on the air at WLIM, speaking with childlike enthusiasm about his "Poppy's music!" A few years back, my sons, Gary and Glenn also helped out and filled in for a few days when I had a brief hospital stay. They handled the show with such professionalism and finesse, that the story was covered by a local paper.

Our listeners have "watched" and heard our children and grandchildren grow up. Many tell me that they love hearing about all of the latest activities and interests in the lives of our family members. At the start of our show, after our traditional first cut featuring Count Basie and our second selection always being Nat King Cole, Dot and I always share the events of the past weekend or any special happenings regarding our children and grandchildren. When I meet listeners, I am always amazed at how much they remember and enjoy the stories about my family! What a joy to not only talk about my family on the air but to now have my children and grandchildren working with us on a regular basis to help produce the show.

While radio and music has been a way of life that I deeply enjoy, my family has always come first... even apart from radio. My family, including my sister Ruth, whom I love so dearly, my wife, my children, my grandchildren, and my many devoted listeners... who have become like family, have all been my continued inspiration.

I believe that our individual definition of "family" and what love is, what good character looks like is based on the examples set for us by our parents and grandparents. My great grandfather, George Washington Shiebler, a once prolific silversmith, was very family oriented and a man of integrity. While I never knew him, an eminent newspaper man once said that in all his career of interviewing "big" people, it was his ... "greatest pleasure, privilege and honor to have met and known that tenderest, most loving and courteous of men, George W. Shiebler."

His son, my granddad, Arthur Moore Shiebler was also a man of integrity. Not only was he very patriotic and cried whenever he watched a parade, he was highly respected in business and recommended as "honest as hell with the nerve of the devil!"

I likewise learned so many values, morals and the meaning of family from my mother's parents, my Grammy and Poppy, who I miss to this day. My father also truly loved his family and had his own wisdom to impart. In a letter that I still have, he once gave me three bits of advice that meant so much to me. He wrote, "First, 'To thine own self be true.' Secondly, always remember your mother, she's your best friend" and last but most important, 'Do unto others as you would have them do unto you'."

This leads me to another driving force in my life, my faith in God. In the 1960's I taught Sunday School for a few years at our church. I was a little hesitant to accept the position and my class consisted of a group of teenagers. It was a challenge in the 60's to keep the attention of teenagers. My main focus was to direct them towards respecting themselves and others and to constantly point them toward the teachings of Jesus. They responded very well and the class was a great time of learning and discussion. Today, after many years of experiencing God's presence and strength in times of crisis, my faith is stronger than ever.

Today, my grandson Michael and I attend a weekly Bible Study taught by our dear family friend, Dr Joseph Harder. Joe Harder has always been there for our family when we have needed prayer and wisdom. Dot and I also regularly tune in to television programs featuring the teachings of Charles Stanley, Joyce Meyer and Greg Laurie. I also enjoy reading the many books written by Billy Graham. I used to watch and enjoy a show with Father John Catoir and the Christophers but I haven't seen it on in a while. John used to interview different prominent guests from various professions. At the end of each interview he would pose the same question to the guest, "Who is Jesus to you?" Every guest had a different and unique answer, some more inspiring than others. One particular gentleman, I think he was a sports figure, had an answer I have never forgotten. When asked, "Who is Jesus to you?" he replied, "He is everything. Without Him, there is nothing." I couldn't agree more.

Regardless of our accomplishments in life or the different paths all of us have chosen, it's amazing how family and faith become even more important as we grow older. I am so thankful for my wonderful family and for the great people I have known, who have taught me by their example of faith.

Dot and I have always appreciated how our listeners enjoy hearing about our family on the air. In almost every show, we still share stories about our children and grandchildren. From the days when we announced the birth of our own children to sharing the joy in the birth of our nine grandchildren, from simple dinners to stories of our beloved pets, our listeners have always loved when we have shared our memories with them. We are so grateful that our radio listening family, has allowed us to be a part of their family.

George W. Shiebler

My great-grandfather, George Washington Shiebler

With Dot at Gary and Linda's wedding -May 1981

Top: Dot and Glenn share a special moment at Glenn and Marilyn's wedding, Sept 1983 - Jim Mooney Photo
Bottom: L-R With Susan, Marilyn, Glenn, Dot, Linda and Gary
Jim Mooney Photo

Dancing with Susan to "Susan Belle" at her wedding, Dec. 1987
Jim Mooney Photo

With Dot, coming up the church aisle after the ceremony
Jim Mooney Photo

Top left: With Dot, our grandchildren and our dog Jeter at
WLIM in 2000
Top right: With sons, Gary and Glenn, 1997.
Bottom: With son Glenn and our grandson Jackson, 2000

Top: With son Gary and granddaughter Hayden -1986
Bottom: With Dot and my sister Ruth - 2009

Dot and I celebrated our 50th anniversary by renewing our vows…with daughter, Susan, son, Glenn and daughter-in-law, Marilyn. - 2001

My grandchildren now lend a hand in helping me create the show! Elissa and I program the music together, Christa is Dot's administrative assistant and Matthew is our producer and assistant DJ - 2012

Our son Gary and our granddaughter Hayden -1996

L-R With my son, Gary, grandchildren, Christa, Michael, Elissa, Matthew and Dot, 2010

With our grandson, Jack- Christmas 2009

With Susan, Gary, Glenn and Dot celebrating my 90th birthday, June 2012

With my niece Hayden, daughter-in-law Linda and Dot

My grandson, Matthew with Dot on the air!

Dot and I with our "adopted" son Ed, (who lived with us for many years) his wife Nancy, Matthew, Elissa Michael and Christa – 2010

Celebrating my 90th birthday with the family! June 2012
L-R back row: With granddaughter Christa, grandson Matthew, son Gary, son Glenn, grandson, Michael
L-R front row: Dot, daughter Susan, my sister Ruth, granddaughters Alice and Elissa

Part III

Famous Friends

Signed photo from Benny Goodman vocalist Peggy Lee.
Inscription: "To Ell, It's been awfully nice knowing you!
Sincerely, Peggy Lee"
Photo credit: Maurice Seymour

HELEN WARD

Helen Ward, a vocalist who sang with Benny Goodman.
Inscription: "To Ell, I'm so lucky - If I hadn't sung with Benny, I would never have met one of the nicest boys I've ever known. Always the best to you - Helen Ward"

Actress, Maureen O'Hara, Inscription, "To Jack, Thank you for your nice letter. Regards, Maureen O'Hara."

One o the world's most renowned drummers - the legendary Gene Krupa, a close friend of mine and Dot's for many years. Inscription: "Thanx, To Jack, my very good friend - Gene Krupa" Photo: James J. Kriegsmann

With leader of the Glenn Miller orchestra (in the 1940's) Tex Beneke during his visit to Providence where Tex and the band were appearing. (Jack Ellsworth, private collection)

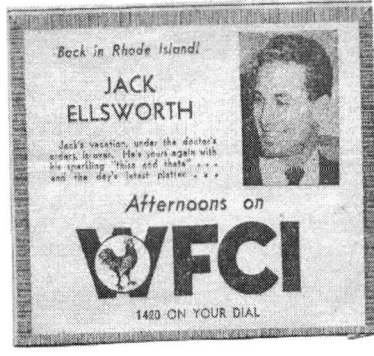

Some early ads featuring yours truly and a 1957 Billboard magazine clipping featuring a special visit with Doris Day in New York City.

FRANCES LANGFORD

   Popular during the 1930's and 1940's, vocalist Frances Langford was the singing star of the Hollywood Hotel Radio program and often worked with friend Dick Powell.
Inscription: "To Jack - Sincerely, Frances Langford"
Photo: Bruno of Hollywood

In a salute to NY broadcasters, Ballantine Beer sponsored a baseball game in 1966 at Yankee stadium featuring NY disc jockeys. I had the ultimate honor of wearing #7, Mickey Mantle's uniform! (I am second from the right in the back row)

In the 1970's, when I was President and General Manager at WALK, I was proud to be on the Board of Directors at Brookhaven Memorial Hospital. L-R Neil Esposito, Mrs. Clifford Hale, Mrs. Walter Vernon, Jack Ellsworth, Francis G. Fosmire (Jack Ellsworth private collection)

Rare photo of orchestra leader and trumpet player Harry James in a April 1972 concert that I emceed at the Greek Church in Blue Point, New York.
Jim Mooney Photo

A special photo with Harry, the same evening.
Jim Mooney Photo

Introducing "Moonlight Serenade" by the Glenn Miller orchestra directed by Buddy DeFranco. Photo was from a performance in 1967. Attached ticket is from a later show in 1972. Jim Mooney Photo.

With leader of the Glenn Miller orchestra, Buddy DeFranco in 1971. Jim Mooney Photo

Emceeing an event with the Larry Elgart Orchestra at Colonie Hill in Hauppauge, NY.
Jim Mooney Photo

With Larry at one of many big band dances which I emceed
Jim Mooney Photo

My interview at Shea Stadium with Mets pitcher Jack Fisher in the early 1960's. That same day I interviewed legend Casey Stengel and Billy Cowan.

Spending some time with former Met's manager Bud Harrelson in 2003 at a fundraiser for children with cancer. (The Sunrise Fund)

> The trustees of
> The Sally Bennett
> **Big Band Hall of Fame Inc.**
> Have Designated
> *Jack Ellsworth*
>
> **Ambassador of Big Band Music**
>
> For perpetuating, promoting and supporting with integrity the sounds of the Big Band Era, the above has earned the title of Big Band Ambassador by the trustees of The Big Band Hall of Fame Inc, West Palm Beach, FL
>
> *Paul Bennett*

What a surprise and honor to receive this distinction!

Dancing with sweetheart Dot at one of many dances we attended in the 1970's
Jim Mooney Photo

With bandleader, Ray Anthony during a visit to our station
WLIM in the 1980's.
Jim Mooney Photo

RAY ANTHONY

Bandleader and trumpet player, Ray Anthony.
Inscription: "To Jack Ellsworth, Thanks for your support. All the Best, Ray Anthony"

With famous singer Jimmy Roselli during a visit to our WLIM studios in the 1980's
Jim Mooney Photo

With my darling wife and partner Dot.

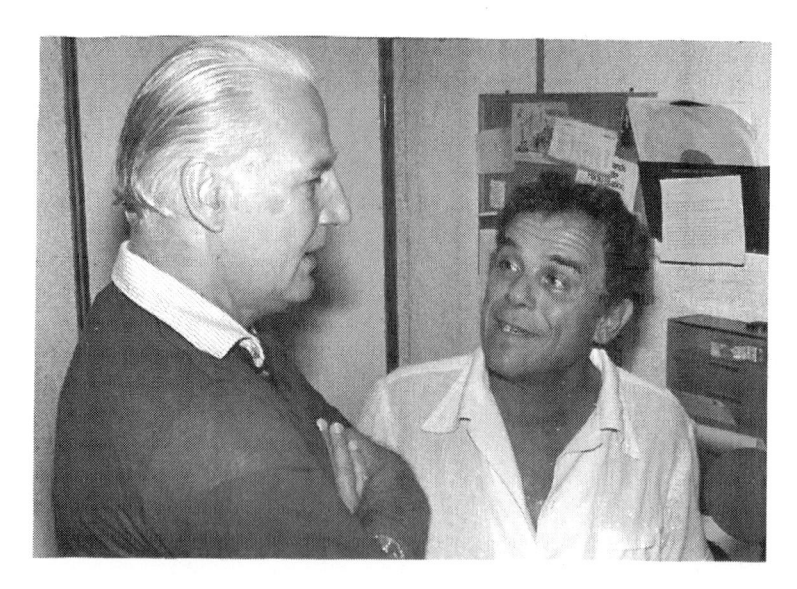

With vocalist Julie La Rosa at WLIM.
Jim Mooney Photo

Great singer, Jerry Vale spending a day with us at WLIM.

With my sweet niece, Lisa Parkman at WLIM.

Publicity photo 1980's

Dancing and celebrating 40 years in radio with my "Dolly."
Felices of Patchogue, Sept 1987.
Jim Mooney Photo

With former County Executive Michael LoGrande, in
September 1987, at my 40th anniversary dinner celebration.
Felices of Patchogue NY.
Jim Mooney Photo

Certificate of Congratulations

Awarded by
The Brookhaven Town Board
to
Jack "Silver Fox" Ellsworth
upon celebrating
50 years of radio broadcasting
at WLIM 1580 AM
serving Brookhaven's 420,000 residents
and in recognition of your fine leadership throughout your career as president
and general manager of WLIM (Patchogue).
Presented from the Town of Brookhaven this 29th day of June, 1997

Eugene Gerrard, *Councilman*

In 1997, I celebrated 50 years in radio!

THE WHITE HOUSE
WASHINGTON

Mr Jack Ellsworth
Village of Bellport
29 Bellport Lane
Bellport, New York 11713

> As you celebrate this special occasion, Hillary and I join your family and friends in extending warmest congratulations. You have our best wishes for every future happiness.
>
> *Bill Clinton*

Imagine the surprise of over 200 guests when this letter was read at my 50th anniversary in radio party! What an honor to receive an acknowledgement from the President of the United States.

Doing what I love most for more than 65 years, bringing the music of the golden era to my listeners! On the air at WALK AM 1370 with my show, "Memories in Melody" - 2012

Actor Gary Cooper, taken to promote the film *Meet John Doe*
1941 Warner Bros. Studios

Movie poster for *Lives of Bengal Lancer* release date January 11,
1935 Courtesy Paramount Pictures

Gary Cooper

"Nan Collins, my manager, came from Gary, Indiana and suggested I adopt that name. She felt it was more exciting than Frank. I figured I'd give it a try. Good thing she didn't come from Poughkeepsie."

~ Gary Cooper

As a kid, I had always admired actor Gary Cooper. His real name was Frank James Cooper but he was known professionally as Gary Cooper. His bio describes him as being "...renowned for his quiet, understated acting style and his stoic, but at times intense screen persona." As a young boy, all I knew was that his movies were among my special favorites. It has been said that he dominated the Hollywood scene for the first twenty years of the talkies. People have always been able to relate to his natural style and to the characters he portrayed.

Gary himself once observed, "To get folks to like you, I figured you had to be their ideal, a fellow who answered their description of a regular guy. People ask me, 'How come you've been around so long'? Well, it's just playing the part of the average American. Until I came along, all the leading men were handsome but luckily, there were a lot of stories about the fellow next door." Gary also once said about a film role he had chosen, "I liked the role because I was portraying a good, sound American character." What a humble, sincere man, the last of the few Hollywood gentleman. In the meantime, Director Henry Hathaway said, "Gary was the most underrated actor I ever worked with." I agree.

There is no disputing, if you have ever seen a Gary Cooper film, you are immediately impressed and the impression is lasting. My favorite Gary Cooper films include "Now and Forever," Mr. Deed's Goes to Town," The Plainsman," "Meet John Doe" and "Pride of the Yankees."

At the tender age of 12, I went to see a movie called, "The Lives of a Bengal Lancer" at the Loew's King's Theatre in Flatbush. Gary Cooper played the role of Lt. MacGregor who died in an attempt to break out of prison in India. His friends were Franchot Tone who played Lt. Forsythe and Richard Cromwell as Lt. Donald Stone. They both survived.

After seeing the film, I decided to write a letter to Gary Cooper. I told him that two friends and I had formed a club based on the film. As children do, we decided as part of the club that we would assume the roles in the film. I was MacGregor and my pals were the other two soldiers.

In my letter to Gary, I complimented him on his acting and the film in general. I also respectfully asked him for some of the materials they used in the film for use in our club. I have added his kind and humorous reply at the end of this chapter.

At only twelve years of age, to receive a letter typed and signed by Gary Cooper on his own letterhead, was the one of the greatest thrills I had ever known. I still cherish the letter, albeit short and to the point, because one of the greatest actors of the 20th century took the time to acknowledge me, just a young fan, in such a kind and personal way.

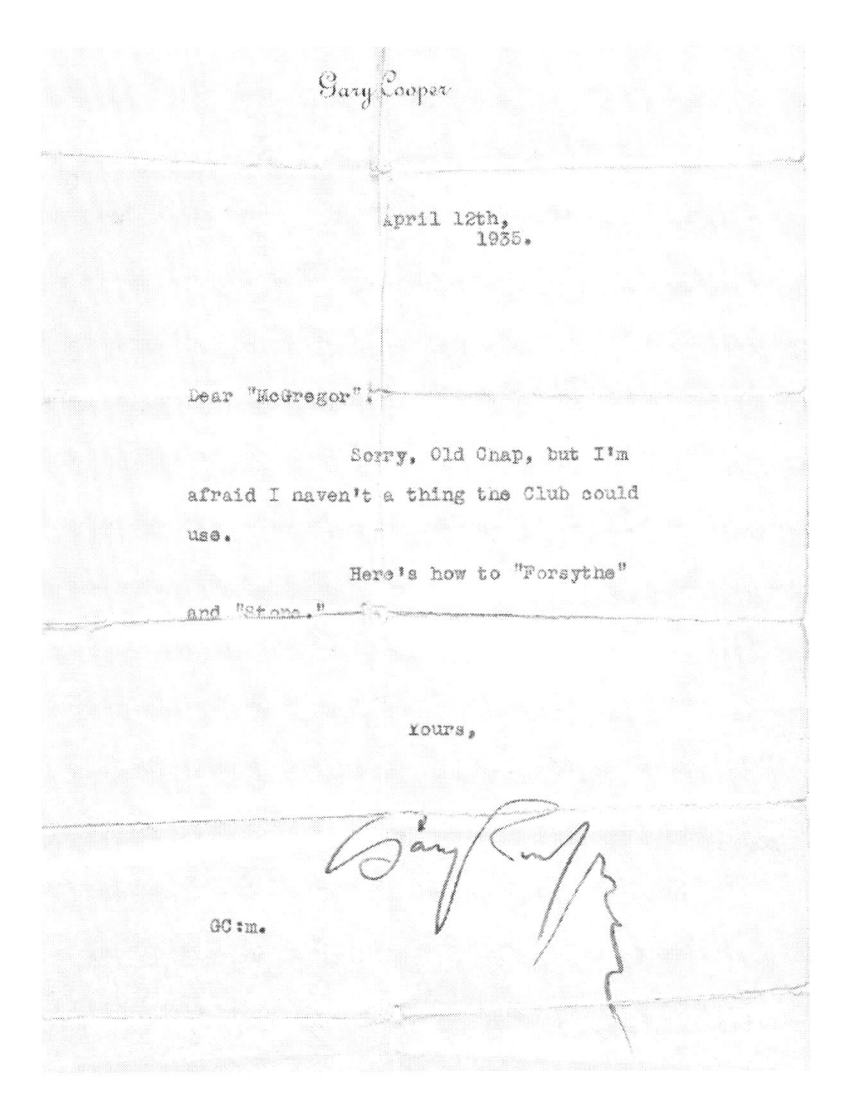

Gary Cooper

April 12th, 1935.

Dear "McGregor":

    Sorry, Old Chap, but I'm afraid I haven't a thing the Club could use.

    Here's how to "Forsythe" and "Stone."

Yours,

Gary Cooper

GC:m.

When I was just 12 years old, this is the wonderful signed letter I received from the great Gary Cooper which reads:

"Dear "McGregor," Sorry Old Chap, but I'm afraid I haven't a thing the Club could use. Here's how to "Forsythe" and "Stone." Yours, Gary Cooper"

Cover of original sheet music from my private collection -1947

Buddy Clark

"Teach us to realize the brevity of life, so that we may grow in wisdom."

~Psalm 90:12 New International Bible

How many of you remember Buddy Clark? He was certainly one of best popular singers of all time. Maybe you will recall some of his hit records. Among the most memorable are "Linda", "Peg O' My Heart', "I'll Dance At Your Wedding", "How Are Things in Glocca Morra", "A Dreamer's Holiday" and "Ballerina." One of his million sellers was "Love Somebody" recorded with Doris day. I once told Doris how much I enjoyed that record. She replied with much enthusiasm, "Oh, I just loved Buddy. He was a joy to work with. What a marvelous sense of humor!" Buddy and Doris recorded several other songs together. I remember, "You Was", " Powder Your Face with Sunshine", "That Certain Party", " My Darling, My Darling" and "I'll String Along With You." Another huge hit for Buddy was the famous recording of "Baby It's Cold

Outside", a duet with Dinah Shore. That one single sold over a million copies! Other records with Dinah Shore included, "Nobody's Home At My House", "My One and Only highland Fling" and "Tea for Two."

In addition to the vocalists who teamed up with Buddy, he made many recordings with the orchestras of Benny Goodman, Eddy Duchin, Wayne King, Xavier Cugat, Mitchell Ayres, Percy Faith, Ray Noble and others. Buddy had several major radio programs. He was once the singing star on Your Hit Parade and was also featured on NBC'S Carnation Contented Hour with Percy Faith's Orchestra and announcer Nelson Case.

I first met Buddy at a Contented Hour rehearsal in 1948. He was most cordial and invited me to join him for a cup of coffee at the Cromwell Drugstore on the lower level of Radio City. As we were heading for the cashier to pay our check, I noticed that someone had dropped a pen on the floor. Buddy was walking ahead of me, looking at a pretty waitress. I said "Hey look Buddy, somebody lost a pen." "Forget the pen," he replied, "Check out that cute mouse!"

Buddy and I became good friends and I'll always remember his kindness when he flew to Providence where I was hosting a disc jockey show. We were starting a new program series from the stage of the Loew's State Theatre. Buddy graciously appeared as a special guest on the initial broadcast and sang several of his hit songs .... all for nothing! The audience was delighted. Later that day we had dinner in the Garden Restaurant at the Hotel Sheraton Biltmore. Bandleader Al Banks learned of Buddy's presence and invited him to come up to sing a couple of songs.. Once again, Buddy graciously obliged.

Born in Boston in 1919, Buddy's earliest ambition was to be a professional baseball player. However, his career plans changed toward a legal career and he entered Northeastern Law School. But Buddy always loved to sing and often performed with local bands. Following service in World War Two, Buddy began a recording career with Columbia Records. Success for this regular, usual kind of guy with an unusual talent was all too brief. The private plane in which he was a passenger crashed on a street in

Los Angeles ending the life of this superb vocalist at the age of only thirty two. Buddy was returning from a football game with several friends. Ironically, he had given up his preferred seat to a woman passenger who survived the crash.

San Francisco disc jockey Jack Carney once observed that, "Buddy Clark sang every song as though his pleasure as a singer was even greater than ours as a listener, whose warmth with a lyric has precluded anyone ever taking his place in the years since his passing. A friend of mine, Jac D'Joseph, an ASCAP composer said that, "Buddy Clark seemed to give a song more melody than it actually had. Listen to Buddy's recordings and tell me one singer who has done them better... no, tell me one singer who has done one of them as well!"

Buddy Clark had a warm, immensely likable personality and a depth of sincerity rare among popular singers. I'm proud to say Buddy was a good friend. I continue to enjoy his recordings and always will. Fortunately, many of the best Buddy Clark performances, originally on 78rpm Columbia records, have been reissued on CDs and can also be found on iTunes.

Buddy Clark was indeed a unique performer who crammed a lot into an all too short life. He left behind many choice examples of how a song should be sung. One of his best recordings says it all, "It Was So Beautiful."

Thank you Buddy. It was beautiful for us too.

My good friend, the great, yet underrated, vocalist Dick Powell
Inscription: "To Sgt. Ell, from citizen Dick Powell" (He likely
meant "civilian" instead of "citizen.")

Dick Powell

"I always insist on truth because there is so much at stake." ~ Dick Powell

"It's been a wonderful life," Dick Powell told me as we sat together reminiscing about his quite incredible career. Once in 1962, when Dick was in New York City for a brief visit, he provided the opportunity for me to tape an interview for my radio program, "Memories in Melody." As a friend of Dick's since the thirties, my purpose in arranging the interview was twofold. I was personally curious to get his opinion on a variety of subjects and I felt listeners would also be interested. Dick Powell crammed an immense amount of success into his 59 years and sadly, when it ended, he was at the peak of his career as an actor-producer and self-described "business man." Dick achieved almost unbelievable success in nearly all aspect of show business. He was almost as successful in real estate

I asked him how it all started and Dick told it this way:

POWELL: It's a pretty long story, Jack. I might sort of skip over it. While I was at Little Rock College back in Arkansas, I sang in church choirs. From there, I went to sing with concert orchestras. Back in 1925, a fellow named Charlie Davis had an orchestra in Indianapolis. I got word he wanted a combination singer and banjo player. I didn't know one banjo string from another, but I figured I could learn so I applied for the job. I told Davis I would report a month later. Then I bought a banjo and taught myself to play. I showed up at the Ohio theatre in Indianapolis on time, but minus most of my fingertips. Later I had my own orchestra and I took the orchestra into theatres and became a master of ceremonies. I remember the very first girl I ever introduced was a pretty but kinda scrawny red-headed kid named Ginger Rogers. She was a Charleston dancer. Then a few years later we did a movie together with Pat O'Brien. It was called Twenty Million Sweethearts. When we first met, co-starring in a motion picture was probably the last thing either of us could have imagined!

J.E: Dick, the people in Pittsburgh often speak of you as though you were a hometown boy. Isn't that so?

POWELL: Yes (smiling). And it makes me feel mighty good too. I worked as a singing master of ceremonies at both the Enright and Stanley theatres in Pittsburgh. I used to sing through a megaphone like Rudy Vallee. That was the closest we came to HI-FI in those days. The people of Pittsburgh always been very good to me and I've always felt right at home there.

J.E: Didn't Hollywood first beckon while you were in Pittsburgh?

POWELL: That's right. A Warner Brothers talent scout wandered into the Stanley theatre one day and caught the show. Next thing I knew I was out in Hollywood making a picture with Lee Tracy called Blessed Event. Then, let's see, I did 42nd Street, The Gold Diggers pictures and oh, about twenty more musicals I think.

J.E.: Ever catch yourself in those old pictures on TV?

POWELL: Oh sure and I sometimes wonder if I was ever really that young!

J.E.: Dick, you kicked around quite a bit before your first break. What advice would you give to young people trying to get into the business?

POWELL: Well, I would say prepare yourself as well as possible. Study and work hard. You know I've always heard those stories about good breaks and being lucky, and I suppose that does have a great deal to do with it. You're lucky if you're born with a certain amount of talent, but the lucky break of getting into something may or may not happen. If you're not prepared, you're certainly not going to stay there after it does happen. So the main thing is hard, hard, hard work.

J.E.: Dick, I've heard people say that your worry a lot. Is there any truth to that?

POWELL: I have heard people refer to me as "a worrier." That's nonsense. Maybe it's because I don't smile all the time…the way they say I used to in pictures. I am always concerned about the quality of my work. Now, maybe that comes across as worrying. Basically, I'm pretty optimistic. You know, like the song says, "There must be happiness ahead!"

J.E.: Your old theme song, of course…that reminds me, even though you've had a tremendous success in dramatic roles, whenever you do a personal appearance and sing a few songs, the applause is deafening. Don't you ever get the yen to sing again on the screen?

POWELL: Well, yes, I do. Honestly, you know that's been such a part of my life [and] I don't think I could ever throw it away. As long as I can squeak out a note I like to sing. I don't think I'd ever make an outright musical anymore, but I might do something with music in it. I really would like to. I wish you'd write me the story!

J.E.: And I wish I were able to. Dick, you certainly had some great songs in those musical pictures…tunes by Dubin and Warren, Arlen and Harburg, Johnny Mercy and Dick Whiting, Irving Berlin and other top writers.

POWELL: I did have some wonderful songs and I still love to sing them because they bring back such fond memories of wonderful people and exciting times. I often think of Ruby Keeler, of the picture I did with Al Jolson years ago, Wonder Bar, [and] the fun I had at Annapolis when we made Shipmates Forever—had a wonderful song in that, "Don't Give Up the Ship." Then the Marine song in The Singing Marine was one of my pet songs. And there was "I'll String Along With You," "I Only Have Eyes For You," "The Shadow Waltz," "Pop Goes Your Heart." Yes, those were some songs!

J.E.: Come to think of it, didn't you make quite a few 'uniform' pictures?

POWELL: Jack, it's strange that you should say that. Actually, I've only made about three uniform pictures. There was Flirtation Walk, Shipmates Forever,…we made a Marine picture. Now, so help me I can't think of another.

J.E.: What about *Page Miss Glory*?

POWELL: Oh well, that was kind of a dreamed-up pilot's uniform.

J.E.: And what about that other one with Marion Davies, Hearts Divided, wasn't it? Weren't you supposed to be a French army officer?

POWELL: Oh, yes. I try to forget that one. That was a bad picture. Yes, I was Napoleon's brother, wasn't I? That was a costume picture. And wait, come to think of it, there was still another uniform. I was a Northwest Mounted Policeman in a picture I did with my own company...Mrs. Mike.

J.E.: You said Hearts Divided was a bad picture. I know you often say you were quite dissatisfied with most of those pictures you did back in the late thirties.

POWELL: I certainly was. I got awfully fed up with those sappy roles they handed me. But I had a contract and I had to learn the script and do what the director said. You just can't argue with the director. Finally, I was able to get out of the rut and since then, things have worked out pretty well for me. It's been a wonderful life.

J.E.: Let's talk a bit about your favorite performers. Who do you like best?

POWELL: First of all, I'm a great fan of June Allyson. I think, really, not only because she's my wife, but she's such a barrel-full of talent, such a wonderful little actress. And then I like Spencer Tracy, Katherine Hepburn, Jim Cagney. And incidentally, I'm delighted with the success of Raymond Burr. I recognized his potential when we first worked together a few years ago in our picture Pitfall. He's a fine actor.

J.E.: What singers do you enjoy most?

POWELL: Well, I'm a great friend and admirer of the old master, Bing. I love to hear Frank Sinatra. I love to hear Perry Como sing. I'm always a great fan of singers because I know sometimes how difficult it is.

J.E.: Dick, how does the Hollywood of today compare with the Hollywood of about thirty years ago when you were a big singing star?

POWELL: Well, it's much more crowded. A lot of young people come to California hoping to break into pictures or television. This has created quite a difficult housing situation and a difficult situation as far as employment is concerned. I know if I were advising anybody who wanted to go to California, I'd certainly say don't go unless you can well afford to because it's growing so fast that they just have more people than they have space...not space but housing. By the way, may I say this? I'm always amazed at the misconceptions so many people have about Hollywood and the actors and actresses. They think everyone has a tremendous home, a big swimming pool, unlimited funds, and a life that consists of one wild party after another. That isn't true at all. Life in Hollywood has changed drastically over the years. Of course, there are a certain few of the so-called big names who, shall we say, don't behave themselves. Their reputations cast a bad light on all of Hollywood. Most of the people I know are real ladies and gentlemen and it's a rotten shame that they have to suffer because of the unsavory reputations of the few.

J.E.: You have known a lot of people in this business. I notice many of the people you worked with at Warner's are now on your TV shows. Nice to see someone who remembers his old friends. Speaking of television, your success in that medium has been nothing short of phenomenal. You've been an actor, director, producer, emcee and an executive. That's really something!

POWELL: Jack, you mentioned five things. Look at your hand. Spread out your fingers. Why restrict yourself to any one? I branched out to protect myself. That way I figure I'll always have a finger or two in the business. Television is a fabulous medium. It has almost no limits. A lot of movie people were afraid of TV when it first came along. They hid their heads in the sand like ostriches. Nobody seemed to want to get in. I thought that I'd better get in somehow or another or be left behind.

J.E.: Dick, you're the busiest man I know so to wrap this up, I'll borrow another of your song titles and say, "Thanks a Million."

POWELL: Thank you, Jack. You've been very nice to me for many years and I've always appreciated it. You know, it does ones' heart good to see his friends do well in life. Believe me, I'm happy and proud of your success in radio. Next time I hope we can spend more time together.

That ended the interview. Later, playing it back, I recalled my first meeting with Dick Powell. Like most teen-aged kids of the thirties, I was an avid movie-goer. The Dick Powell-Ruby Keeler musicals with the lavish Busby Berkeley production numbers and girls, girls, girls represented my idea of the ultimate in entertainment.

In 1936, my dad Howard A. Shiebler, who was working with George White on sketches for his Scandals Broadway show, told me that he and White had been talking to Dick Powell about a starring role in the '36 Scandals. "You really talked with Dick Powell?" I gasped. "I wish I could meet that guy sometime."

Unfortunately, Dick's trip East was a brief one and no introduction was possible at that time. As I understood it (and this isn't common knowledge), Dick wanted very much to star in the Scandals but his Warner Brothers contract made it impossible. Eventually, Rudy Vallee was signed and did his customary capable job, but it has always seemed a shame that Dick's career couldn't have included a starring role in at least one Broadway musical. He was a natural for it.

The introduction I sought did come several years later while Dick was In new York rehearsing for a CBS radio show. The show was "Tune Up Time" with Wendy Barrie and the Kay Thompson singers. Mike Foster, CBS publicity man, took me backstage and I met Dick Powell. He was just as nice as pie and I'll never forget his genuinely sincere interest in a kid who had nothing more to offer than great admiration.

I remember telling Dick that I liked Ginger Rogers, and he told me she was the prettiest girl in pictures. We also talked baseball. I liked the Brooklyn Dodgers and he was a Pittsburgh Pirates fan.

Dick also told me even then of his aspirations to do something more meaningful in pictures. In fact, he and Wendy Barrie did a suspenseful bit on the show that evening. Later Dick sang a new tune, Hoagy Carmichael's "I Get Along Without You Very Well."

And so that was the beginning of a twenty-four year friendship. I have many pleasant memories of Dick Powell. The most vivid of all is the memory of a visit at his North Hollywood home in 1944 while I was in the U.S. Marines. I was stationed at Camp Elliott in San Diego. While on a weekend pass, I telephoned Dick and he invited me to his home. The first thing he did when I walked in the door was to sit down and write a letter to my parents to tell them I was well.

"We will enjoy his visit," he wrote, "especially my children who will probably drive him mad with questions about the Marines. His being a three striper will mean an awful lot because my son says the most important people in this war are sergeants. That's all, just wanted to say hello to you for him."

During my visit Dick took me on the grand tour of Hollywood, including a visit to the RKO set of his new picture Murder, My Sweet. Between takes, I met the cast and at lunch Ann Shirley offered me a bite of her hot dog. I took it, lipstick on the roll and all!

When we left the studio, Dick was surrounded by a mob of girls seeking his autograph. As he obliged, Dick grinned, "You know you'd rather get Frank Sinatra!"

Yes, I have many wonderful memories of Dick Powell. I wonder how many people realize what a huge gap has been left in show business since his passing. This was not just another guy who, aside from his business acumen, got lucky and hit it big. This was a true show business phenomenon in the tradition of Jolson, Crosby and Garland. I never felt his talent as a singer and musical comedy start were properly utilized in pictures, at least not consistently. I blame this on a combination of things. He suffered from the worst kind of type-casting, weak, tiresome hack plots, often bad directions and a misconceived notion of what the public really wanted. The "backstage at the musical" bit was great for the first few films but like Westerns on TV, the familiar pattern was grossly overworked.

Those under seventy probably won't remember, but anyone who saw Dick in his best musical films, in the Pittsburgh days or in person at the New York Paramount, the Capitol Theatre in the forties, will remember the man for the great showman that he was. There was the warm smile that could light up a stage, the clear, lilting voice, the roguish gleam in the eye, the overall impression of a performer who just glowed with talent, personality and charm.

On a stage, Dick could tell a great story. He played a sax, clarinet and a trumpet, and he played them well; but above all, the audience waited for him to sing. When Dick ran out on the stage, threw out his arms and burst into, "Over the sea, let's go men...," pr "Oh baby what I couldn't do—oo—oo with plenty of money and you," you knew here was a star!

The whole take of the guy was dynamic and exciting. I don't think we'll ever see his equal. In a 1937 movie magazine, Dick Powell was described as follows: "He's a born entertainer and is as much at home before a mike as before a camera. Yet, in all Hollywood, he is the least conceited." In the next quarter of a century of almost unparalleled success that reputation never changed.

My grandfather was a lovable old gent who travelled through every state in the nation. In the old days he worked in silent films and met thousands of people in his eighty-some-odd years. He was a discerning judge of character. Although he never met Dick Powell, Granddad never missed his motion pictures or his radio shows. He once put it this way: "I like Dick Powell because he is always such a gentleman."

Could anyone have said it better?

Dick Powell

Jan. 15, 1944

Dear Mr & Mrs Shiebler;

Your son Ell is here in my house for the night, having arrived a few hours ago from San Diego. I just thought that you would like to know that he is well and looks fine. He called today and I invited him to stay here with us. He's a fine boy and we will enjoy his visit, especially my children who will probably drive him mad with questions about the Marines. He being a three striper will mean an awfully lot because my son says the most important people in this war are Seargents. That's all, just wanted to say hello to you for him.

Please accept my very best wishes for your continued health and happiness,

Sincerely,

Dick Powell

Dear Folks,
I'm having a life long dream come true here with Dick. He certainly is being swell to me and it will take a whole letter about five pages long to fully describe this experience. Will write in a day or so. Gosh – this is it! Love, Ell

My handwritten note at the end of Dick's letter: "I'm having a lifelong dream come true here with Dick. He certainly is being swell to me and it will take a whole letter about five pages long to fully describe this experience. Will write in a day or so. Gosh – this is it! Love, Ell"

Inscription:
To "Ell" Best Wishes, Dick Powell

DICK POWELL

3-9-49

Mr Jack Ellsworth

Babylon, Long Island
New York

Dear Ell,

Thanks for your letter. I'm glad you liked the pictures.

We are starting MRS MIKE March 21 and I hope it goes all right. So far, we don't know who the girl is to be.

Tell your grandmother many thanks and you may also tell her that I'm probably going to make a picture this fall with a few songs in it. If you have an idea for a story send it to me.

Thanks again for your note and here's best wishes,

Dick
Dick Powell

DP:tk

Inscription: "To 'Ell' Thanks & very best wishes- Dick Powell"
Photo: Victogaph Inc. (Jack Ellsworth private collection)

DICK POWELL

209 Copa de Oro
Los Angeles 24, Calif.
May 11, 1948

Mr. Jack Ellsworth
  Custom House
St. Providence 3, R. I.

Dear Ell:

    Well Congratulations! From the looks of the brochure you sent me you are really doing fine. Also thanks for the comments and plugs on "To the Ends of the Earth". Needless to say I always appreciate the nice things you do for me.

    I think you are very wise to continue going to school. Keep up the good work!

    You can rest assured that if I ever get in your neighborhood I shall be sure to give you a call.

    Thanks again for your letter, I am,

                    Sincerely,

                    Dick Powell

DP:pg

"To Ell, With best wishes and appreciation of your friendship. Sincerely, Dick Powell"

Signed photo from Benny- Inscription: "To Ell, In appreciation, a real fan, a swell guy, Benny"
Photo credit: Maurice Seymour

Benny Goodman

"Sometimes when you start losing detail, whether it's in music or in life, something as small as failing to be polite, you start to lose substance."

~ Benny Goodman

    I doubt if there is a more devoted Benny Goodman enthusiast anywhere in the world than yours truly. Enjoying those early Goodman records was an important part of my teenage years. However, having the opportunity to actually meet and get to know the man more fully intensified my interest in this icon.

I first met Benny in 1942 when he was appearing at the Terrace Room of the hotel New Yorker. I had become friendly with vocalist Art Lund who introduced me to the great Mr. Goodman. I noticed at once that Benny was not an outgoing person. When we first met, he merely smiled and shook my hand. Sometime later, when he noticed me night after night standing in front of that mesmerizing band, totally immersed in his music, he became increasingly cordial.

I am convinced that whenever performers realize that someone is a genuinely sincere admirer, they respond in kind. Benny was well aware of my great interest in his band and his brilliant mastery of the clarinet in particular. I was, and still am, totally enthralled and entranced with his unparalleled technique and skill on the clarinet. Bandleader, Woody Herman once remarked, "A lot of us play the clarinet but Benny is the only one who really knows how to do it!"

Benny had complete mastery of his instrument and could play jazz and classical music with equal dexterity. Quoting from a publicity release in the early eighties: "Benny Goodman and his clarinet changed the way we listen to music. Forget the nostalgia, the legend and the history because for six decades he produced the purest, most ecstatic sounds ever raised."

Singer Art Lund was probably the best male vocalist ever to be a part of the Benny Goodman Orchestra, both before and after, World War II. Art later went out on his own to record the million seller, "Mamselle" and later to success on Broadway.

As much as he admired Benny, Art knew that the maestro was often forgetful and absent-minded. He once told me this story. During the time when the Goodman Band was appearing at the Hotel New Yorker, there was a dinner break between nine and ten. Benny often left the hotel while most of the band members had a quick meal and then returned to the band room directly behind the band stand.

One evening, shortly before ten, Benny entered the band room and seeing a group of musicians sitting and chatting he called out, "Hey you guys, we have a set to play. Let's get out on the stand!' One of the men stood up and said, "Hey, wait a minute Benny! We are not with your band. We're with Jimmy Dorsey over at the Pennsylvania. We just came over to say hello to your guys" Since both Benny's and Dorsey's musicians were wearing maroon jackets, Benny was momentarily confused. But Art said this was no unusual for the King of Swing who was so involved and preoccupied with this music and focused that he was sometimes unaware of what was going on in the world around him.

Those who worked with Benny often complained about his absent-mindedness and his expectation that everyone should play as well as he did. Vibraphone player, Red Norvo once said, "Because nobody was on a par with Benny's talent, you know he couldn't help being demanding." I always felt that the intriguing thing about Benny was that he never recognized that people didn't have as much ability as he did. He always thought everybody should be just as great as he was. He didn't think too much of it really. I don't consider him a very conceited guy or anything....he'd look at guys and say, 'What's the matter with you?' ...and they were thinking, "My God!'"

Frank Sinatra told a friend that he once said to Benny, "Everytime I saw you Ben, we were together and you were constantly noodling. (practicing) I asked him, 'Why do you do that constantly?' His reply was, 'Because if I'm not great, I'm good'."

Jazz writer Will Friedwald, relates an example of how highly another legendary jazz player regarded Benny. One night in 1940, Red Norvo ran into Charlie "Bird" Parker and asked if there was anything he could do for him? "Yeah, said Bird, "Get me into see Benny Goodman!"

I had the the great fortune to hear Benny at many places in the metropolitan area, primarily the New Yorker Hotel in 1942 and

1943. I also caught the king at the mosque theater in Newark, at the Westchester County Center, at the Rainbow Grill atop Rockefeller Center and of the course at the New York Paramount. What a thrill to see and hear that great band playing "Let's Dance" on the rising stage!

What a thrill it has been, and continues to be, just being even a small part of the entertainment world. In nearly six decades I have been privileged to meet and get to know many of the "Greats" in show business. Benny Goodman was a special favorite. Famous for being introverted, reticent and preoccupied with his music, he knew of my great admiration and affection and we became good friends. In 1973 I had the rare opportunity of interviewing Benny at his New York apartment. His answers demonstrate his candid opinions and reflect his personality and views at that time. Discussion of a recording released at the time of the interviews led to the first general question about working with a small group versus the Big Band.

JE: Is there as much rehearsal required with a small group as with the Big Band?

BG: Well there's a certain amount of rehearsal. Of course, you don't have any music...you don't have any arrangements that are written, contrary to a Big Band. In a Big Band you have charts, you know. You know exactly what you're going to do, more or less, and you get down all the phrasing for the saxophones and the brass and so forth. It takes a good deal of rehearsal, but with a small group you haven't anything like that; you just have to be able to play well and suggest ideas....different little riffs and beginnings and endings of arrangements and that kind of thing. That's about all.

JE: Each time it's quite different.

BG: That's right. You have all that freedom. You have complete freedom.

JE: This must be more enjoyable for you.

BG: It can be, yes.

JE: You've had many bands since the thirties. Is there one band you liked the best?

BG: Well, I think they're all quite different. The band we had at the Palomar Ballroom. There was a great warmth for the band right away. That was in 1935.

JE: Have you noticed popular music today taking any particular directions?

BG: I can't very well analyze it. I do think there's a conglomeration. Every once in a while a perfectly nice song will come along and be a big hit, and that was true many years ago too. Some song like, "I Will Wait For You." There are quite a few of Burt Bachrach's...I'm interested in his music, but I'm only interested in the ones you can improvise upon, and there aren't too many of those.

JE: You've done recordings over and over again to get just the right one. Do you recall the largest number of takes you've done on a record?

BG: Well, I suppose what that comes from (the penchant for perfection) can be explained because as a rule I would play these songs at the hotel. We played all these tunes and the band had a chance to warm up. At some point we were really in the groove, so to speak and a particular arrangement would really come off. And now you get in the studio on a cold morning in a totally different atmosphere and you're trying to recreate what you did a couple of nights before. It's just as simple as that, and sometimes you might overplay your hand.

JE: That's why airchecks are so great. You have excitement you don't get in a cold studio.

BG: Well, I think that's very necessary for a band that's supposed to swing.

JE: Benny, it's been said that you can always tell a Benny Goodman band by the way it swings. What's the secret of making that happen?

BG: Well, I don't think there is any trick to it. I've always been interested in what makes things happen in music... what you have to do from the point of view of technique, of guiding musicians. I think it's basically a musical approach, how to make a crescendo, how to make a forte, how to make a pianissimo, how to make a point in music. I think that's what really makes it swing. Actually, the things one learns from a textbook.

JE: Do you listen to many of the bands today? Are there any you particularly like?

BG: I think Don Ellis. I heard him on a television show and was quite taken with him.

JE: What jazz clarinetist do you more admire?

BG: Buddy De Franco is a brilliant clarinet player. I always liked Pete Fountain's playing very much...Barney Bigard, Jimmy Hamilton...quite a few.

JE: Do you practice regularly?

BG: Very much so.

JE: You're mature and not traveling and working as much as you used to.

BG: In that case you've got to practice more. Oh, at least an hour a day. Your lip, your technique, you get rusty.

JE: Do you still get a thrill playing before an audience and watching their reaction?

BG: I think so. Well the excitement....I think both work with you...or just one?

BG: Rachel used to. She used to play piano with me; we'd be in concert together.

JE: Thanks very much for giving us so much time.

    I saw Benny at Carnegie Hall the second time he performed there and again at many broadcast rehearsals and performances. An unforgettable night for me was in April of 1973 when the Benny Goodman sextet appeared at the Knights of Columbus Hall in Patchogue, NY. Every time Benny was appearing in New York, he always sent me an invitation.

    Benny and I remained friends until his death on June 13, 1986 which, by sad coincidence, occurred on my birthday. One of the highlights in our relationship took place in May of 1982 when Benny celebrated his birthday with us at WLIM. We devoted the entire day to Benny Goodman recordings. When I asked him how he felt about a full day of Benny Goodman music, he smiled and said, "Well If you can take it, I guess I can too!"

    To me, Benny was the greatest jazz instrumentalist of all time and without question the catalyst of the swing era. However, aside from witnessing the musical genius of this man over a lifetime, I think I feel even more blessed to have known him personally. A man who was somewhat reclusive, private and almost stoic, regarded me as a trustworthy friend.

It's almost as much of a gift as the music he gave the world. Benny, we miss you.

Benny and Frances Langford in Hollywood Hotel- 1937

Photo credit: Vitagraph Inc.

Benny at the Camel Caravan rehearsal, NY 1937... Even to a genius like Benny Goodman, music can be fun!

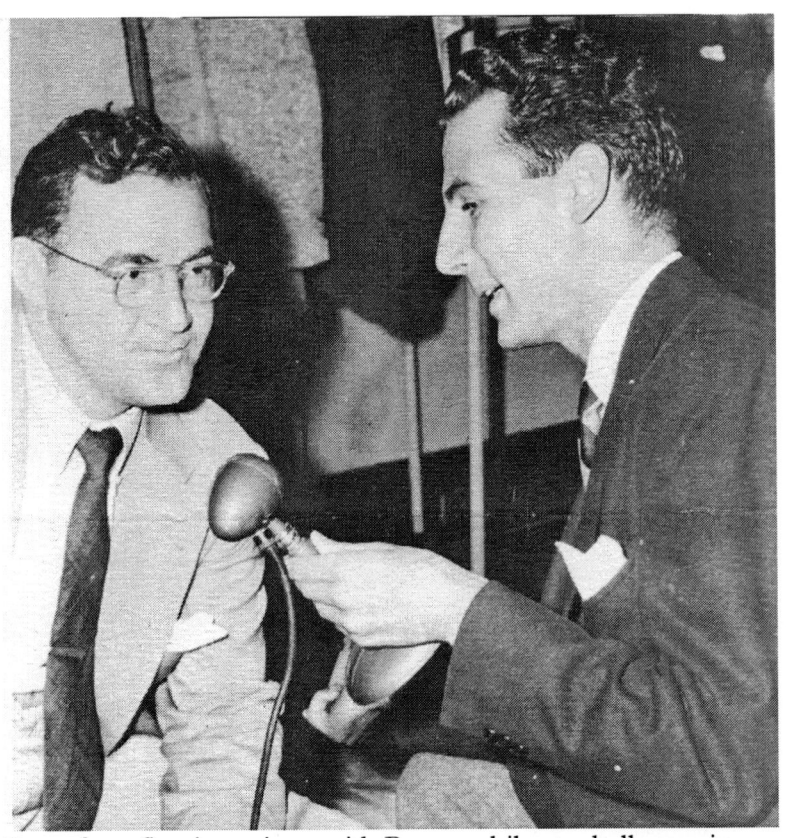

One of my first interviews with Benny while at a ballroom in Providence, Rhode Island. - 1948

Rare photo of Benny in Central Park, NY for a war bond drive benefit performance- 1943

Benny with Dot while visiting our WLIM studios to celebrate his birthday in 1982.
Jim Mooney Photo

Blowing out birthday candles with Benny! Jim Mooney Photo

Benny with George Drake, yours truly and Dot at WLIM 1982
Jim Mooney Photo

Benny Goodman performing at Carnegie Hall, 1938

Remembering Benny Goodman's Carnegie Hall Concert

"In bringing jazz to Carnegie, Benny Goodman was, in effect, smuggling American contraband into the halls of European high culture, and Goodman and his 15 men pulled it off with the audacity and precision of Ocean's Eleven." ~ Will Friedwald

    If you are a Benny Goodman fan, you are surely familiar with his now famous 1938 Carnegie Hall concert. Benny Goodman was initially reluctant to perform there but, once he was committed, he dedicated himself to its success. He gave up other performances so he could hold rehearsals inside the famous New York concert hall to become fully acquainted with the venue and its rich acoustics.

Much to Benny's surprise, the concert sold out two weeks prior to the night of the show. Carnegie Hall's seating capacity was 2,760 seats and tickets were on sale for $2.75 a seat. It may seem like nothing now but in January of 1938 that was quite an expense. By the end of the evening, there were requests for an encore and five curtain calls. Benny Goodman's concert was surely a success an he now had the distinction of being the first jazz bandleader to perform at Carnegie Hall. After years of working for some acknowledgement and more respectability, jazz had finally been accepted by mainstream audiences.

In 1943, I was a sergeant in the U.S. Marine Corps stationed briefly at the Brooklyn Navy Yard.
Benny's former vocalist, Helen Ward was singing with Hall McIntyre's orchestra at the New York Strand Theatre. I met Helen for lunch and she introduced to recording executive and financier Albert Marx who was her ex-husband. Helen and Benny Goodman had a brief romance at one time and he came very close to proposing marriage to her. However, according to Helen, he called it off at the last minute, citing his career. A year or so later, Albert Marx greatly angered Benny Goodman when Helen left the band to marry him.

One evening in the spring of 1945, Albert graciously invited me to his home in Rye, N.Y. where he played his 78 RPM acetates of the now famous 1938 Benny Goodman Carnegie Hall Concert. Marx had arranged for Goodman's Carnegie Hall concert to be recorded for Helen as an anniversary present. Albert also played some choice air checks of the '37 band.

Naturally, I was thrilled beyond belief especially to hear the Carnegie Hall sides, recorded from a single overhead mic not far from stage left. This accounts for the extra prominence of Krupa's drums and the excellent sound of Jess Stacy's piano. Albert somewhat reluctantly let me borrow the discs. I took them home and played them for some friends and they were completely blown away as I had been! The sound was magnificent.

In 1947, at my first radio job at WHIM in Providence, I had now had my own copy of the concert and couldn't resist playing the entire concert on the air. The audience reaction was enormous!

I feel so honored to be one of the first to ever hear the recordings of this extraordinary event in the history of Benny Goodman and Carnegie Hall. The concert was indeed a major musical event. Already proclaimed as the "King of Swing" and acknowledged as the catalyst of the swing era, Benny Goodman made musical history delighting both jazz and concert music lovers with his precedent shattering performance.

Goodman's band featured soloists included Gene Krupa, Harry James, Jess Stacy, Ziggy Elman, Teddy Wilson and Lionel Hampton. Pretty Martha Tilton sang two songs, "Loch Lomond" and "Bei Mir Bist du Schön." She was a vision in her pink party dress.

The band sparkled on such Goodman favorites as "Don't Be That Way," "One O'Clock Jump," "Swingtime in the Rockies" and "Sing, Sing Sing." Performances by the famous Goodman quartet also delighted the audience.

The Columbia recordings of the concert continue to be best sellers for those who remember the era and for young people who are discovering the excitement for the first time. It is almost impossible to listen and not be thrilled.....almost seventy-five years later!

Complimentary Souvenir
World's Most Famous Jazz Concert
January 16, 1938

CARNEGIE HALL PROGRAM
SEASON 1937-1938

FIRE NOTICE—Look around *now* and choose the nearest exit to your seat. In case of fire walk (not run) to *that* Exit. Do not try to beat your neighbor to the street.

JOHN J. McELLIGOTT, *Fire Commissioner*

CARNEGIE HALL

Sunday Evening, January 16th, at 8:30

S. HUROK

presents

(by arrangement with Music Corporation of America)

BENNY GOODMAN
and his
SWING ORCHESTRA

I.

"Don't Be That Way" .... *Edgar Sampson*
"Sometimes I'm Happy" (from "Hit the Deck") .... *Irving Caesar & Vincent Youmans*
"One O'clock Jump" .... *William (Count) Basie*

II.

TWENTY YEARS OF JAZZ

"Sensation Rag" (as played c. 1917 by the Dixieland Jazz Band)
E. B. Edwards

PROGRAM CONTINUED ON SECOND PAGE FOLLOWING

— NOT FOR SALE —

My rare copy of the original program

PROGRAM CONTINUED

•

"I'm Comin Virginia" (as played c. 1926 by "Bix" Beiderbecke)
Cooke-Heywood
"When My Baby Smiles at Me" (as played c. 1927 by Ted Lewis)
Munro-Sterling-Lewis
"Shine" (as played c. 1929 by Louis Armstrong) *Mack-Brown-Dabney*
"Blue Reverie" .... *Duke Ellington*
"Life Goes to a Party" .... *Harry James-Benny Goodman*

III.

JAM SESSION
    Collective improvision by a group of soloists to be announced. The length of the session is indeterminate, and may include one or more tunes.

IV.

"Tiger Rag" .... *Nick La Rocca*
"Body and Soul" .... *John Green*

    The Goodman Trio
    Teddy Wilson, *Piano*
    Gene Krupa, *Drums*
    Benny Goodman, *Clarinet*

PROGRAM CONTINUED ON SECOND PAGE FOLLOWING

V.

"Avalon" .... *Al Jolson-Vincent Rose*

"The Man I Love" (from "Strike Up the Band")
George and Ira Gershwin

"I Got Rhythm" (from "Girl Crazy") .... *George and Ira Gershwin*
The Goodman Quartet
Wilson, Krupa, Goodman and Lionel Hampton, *Vibraphone*

—— *Intermission* ——

VI.

"Blue Skies" .... *Irving Berlin*
"Loch Lomond" .... *Traditional Scotch*

VII.

"Blue Room" (from "The Girl Friend") .... *Richard Rodgers and Lorenz Hart*

"Swingtime in the Rockies" .... *James Mundy*

"Bei Mir Bist du Schoen" .... *Jacobs-Secunda-Cahn-Chaplin*

VIII.

"Who" (from "Sunny") .... *Jerome Kern-Otto Harbach*
"Dinah" .... *Harry Akst*
"Stompin' at the Savoy" .... *Edgar Sampson*
"I'm a Ding Dong Daddy" .... *Phil Baxter*
Goodman Trio and Quartet

PROGRAM CONTINUED ON PAGE 12

IX.
"Sing, Sing, Sing" .... Louis Prima

X.
Reprise

•

Baldwin Piano Used

•

The Program is Subject to Slight Alteration

•

Members of the Orchestra
  Benny Goodman, *Clarinet*

    Reeds: Babe Rusin, George Koenig, Herman Shertzer and Arthur Rollini
    Trumpets: Harry James, Ziggy Elman and Gordon Griffin
    Trombones: Red Ballard and Vernon Brown
    Harry Goodman, *Bass;* Allan Reuss, *Guitar;* Jess Stacy, *Piano;* Gene Krupa, *Drums;* Martha Tilton, *Vocalist*

    Cornet soloist in "I'm Comin' Virginia": Bobby Hackett

    Soloists in "Blue Reverie": Johnny Hodges, *Soprano Saxophone;* "Cootie" Williams, *Trumpet;* and Harry Carney, *Baritone Saxophone*

•

Guest soloists in the Jam Session:
  Count Basie, *Piano*
  Lester Young, *Tenor Saxophone*
  "Buck" Clayton, *Trumpet*
  Freddie Green, *Guitar*
  Walter Page, *Bass*
  Johnny Hodges, *Alto Saxophone*
  Harry Carney, *Baritone Saxophone*
    and
  Members of the Goodman Orchestra

•

This performance by courtesy of the Hotel Pennsylvania

•

Concert Management: HUROK ATTRACTIONS, Inc.
30 Rockefeller Plaza, N. Y. C.

The one and only Glenn Miller

Glenn Miller

"A band ought to have a sound all of its own. It ought to have a personality." ~ Glenn Miller

"Overwhelmingly beautiful." That description of Glenn Miller's music comes from a fellow musician, saxophonist Phil Bodner. Glenn's famous theme "Moonlight Serenade" vividly recalls those years from the late 1930's to the 1940's when the big bands reigned supreme in the world of popular music. It has been called "The "Golden Era."

There are many ways to describe Glenn's music...evocative, poignant, ineffably touching and forever memorable. Musicologist Gunther Schuller wrote "One has to go outside western culture to Japanese Gaguku or Hindu music to find a sound so singularly distilled and unvaryingly consistent in its use."

In his definitive book, "The Big Bands", George T. Simon says "Of all the outstanding popular dance bands, the one that evokes the most memories of how wonderfully romantic it all was, the one whose music people most want to hear over and over again, is the band of the late Glenn Miller. This was a band of great moods, of great contrasts, of great excitement." My favorite description of the Miller sound comes from John S. Wilson, the famous New York Times critic, record reviewer and one of the most knowledgeable and respected writers in the world of popular music. John said "It was a magical sound that Glenn Miller created, a sound that lifted you up out of your everyday world, carried you to the clouds, whirled you toward heaven and bathed all your daydreams in the warmest romantic glow you had ever known. It had a sparkle too, a bright, happy feeling that added an extra tingle to your joy."

The warm, mellow singing of the reeds, the rich sonority of the trombones, the jaunty joy of those rhythm tunes....they were all woven into a musical magic carpet in those few short years that the Miller Band played just before World War II.

Glenn's long time friend and former leader of Glenn's post-war band, Ray McKinley said: "There's only one word to think of to call the Glenn Miller sound....Magic! "Those of us who knew Glenn Miller, who played with him, saw him in that great desire for perfection, Rehearsing one phrase hundreds of times until it was right is no press agent's concoction. Discipline and determination were bywords for Glenn. Sometimes a few of the boys couldn't see the sense in going over and over some some part of a song until the actual performance when the dancers instead of dancing, formed a sort of giant half moon in front of the bandstand and listened to the Miller sound, a clarinet playing the melody an octave above the tenor sax, with additional saxophones playing the harmony. If that's not magic ...I don't know what is."

Johnny Mince, a good friend and famed clarinetist, once lived in Blue Point and gave clarinet lessons to our sons Gary and Glenn and flute lessons to our daughter Susan. Johnny at one time was featured with the great Tommy Dorsey band while Glenn

Miller was with Ray Noble. Glenn told Johnny about an exercise he had written for his music teacher. They decided to record it on May 23 at New York's Harry Smith recording studio. The band consisted of three clarinets, three violins and a guitar. There were four movements to the work with what was to become an ongoing theme throughout. The theme had several title changes until the spring of 1939 when it finally became the now famous, "Moonlight Serenade." Dave Garroway once described it as "America's second national anthem."

Johnny also told me that his boss, Tommy Dorsey, would be furiously jealous when he learned that Glenn Miller and his orchestra had broken an attendance record at a theatre or ballroom where Tommy's band had previously had the record crowds...and it happened more than once. The often volatile Dorsey would wail,"What the hell does he have that we haven't?"

Here's another Glenn Miller story, this one from Glenn's "Boy Singer" Ray Eberle. Ray told me that often when he would report to the RCA recording studios for a morning recording session, he was assigned a number of new songs that were unknown to him. Ray said that before the recording began, Glenn would take him into the men's room, take his trombone out of the case, put one foot up on the sink and play the melody a few times. He used to say, "Heres how it goes Jim." (Glenn often called Ray "Jim" telling him that he didn't look like a "Ray.") Ray said he learned a lot of songs that way.

Everyone is familiar with such Miller songs as "In The Mood", "String of Pearls" and "Chattanooga Choo Choo" and those original recordings sell today as though they were current hits. Travel anywhere on this earth and you will hear dance bands still trying to copy the Glenn Miller style. Why has it lasted? What is there about the music of Glenn Miller that has given it this unique appeal?

Glenn Miller's band played at a time when the world was on the verge of change, and it caught and preserved something of value in such a meaningful way that it has survived the rigors of that change. In retrospect, the world was young and innocent when Glenn Miller played his music. It was music that sang of wonder and hope and happiness and the magic of the Miller sound...the true magic of that sound......is just that. Even though the world has changed, Glenn Miller's music still touches those responsive chords that lift our spirits and stir the glowing embers of romance. You can still hear that magic...all you have to do is listen.

A great Glenn Miller fan, former President Ronald Reagan had this to say when he once hosted a big band special broadcast back in the late fifties... "Of all the bands that made movies, the most successful was that of Glenn Miller. Just as crowds flocked to hear his band at the Glen Island Casino or the local ballroom when they played in our home town, we all saved our allowance to buy his records. Every youngster was sure to rush to see Glenn's movies." Do you remember "Orchestra Wives" and "Sun Valley Serenade"?

There was something very special about Glenn Miller...he had a businesslike, orderly approach to life which was reflected in his music. The Miller band never looked sloppy....never played sloppy. Glenn rarely socialized with band members, except for pianist and longtime friend, Chummy McGregor. However, Glenn was extremely attentive to his fans. One of our radio listeners, Madeleine Neenan of Mount Sinai, told me that one Saturday afternoon, she and a girlfriend went to New York City to see a movie. Before catching the train home, they stopped at the Pennsylvania Hotel where Glenn was conducting his "Sunset Serenade" broadcast. As they walked up the entrance of the Cafe Rouge, Glenn was just stepping out for a break between sets. He approached the awestruck duo and said, "Hello Girls! I bet I know what you would like... an autograph from Ray Eberle." Excitedly, they accompanied Glenn to the bandstand where Ray obliged. Madeleine asked Glenn if he would autograph the top of her white pleated skirt. When he hesitated, she quickly explained, "It's okay, I have another one at home!" Needless to say, she never wore that skirt again.

In 1955, I wrote a letter to Don Haynes, Glenn's close friend and his executive officer. Don had been Glenn's personal manager during their civilian careers. I asked Don when he recognized the band's great potential? He replied that it was, "...in the summer of

1939 at the Glen Island Casino in New Rochelle." I asked him to name his favorite Miller record. he picked "Tuxedo Junction."

Finally I wrote: There are many stories and rumors circulating. What, in your honest opinion, is the true story of Glenn's disappearance? Here are Don's exact words: "His plane a singled-motored C-64, no doubt went down in the English Channel as it had no de-icing equipment. I put him on the plane and fully believe that is what happened...there were countless rumors but all of them baseless."

But some real magic has even happened in the years since then. Many years have passed since Glenn Miller led his band for the last time. Yet the magic of the Miller sound lives on, still fresh, still inviting, with an appeal that has defied time, geography and the fate of most popular fancies: a quick trip to oblivion. One reason it has lived on is due to people who have kept the magic alive, great people, like Larry O'Brien. My wife and I first heard about Larry O'Brien in the 1990's. We were astounded at the job he was doing leading the Glenn Miller Orchestra. Not only was he a great conductor but like Glenn, a great trombone player. Larry was always so enthusiastic about the Glenn Miller sound. Not only did Larry keep that great sound alive, he has a rich musical history of his own. Larry was associated with big bands earlier in his career. He performed with the great orchestras of Sammy Kaye, Buddy Morrow, Ralph Marterie, Ray Eberle, Billy May, Les Elgart, Boyd Raeburn, Art Mooney, and Lee Castle, not to mention playing with the Al Ramsey Orchestra at Ceasar's Palace, backing up such stars as Tom Jones and Frank Sinatra. He also worked with Sergio Franchi, Wayne Newton, Roy Clark, and many other noted performers.

In 2006, I emceed a Glenn Miller Orchestra event at the Patchogue NY Theatre to benefit the Sunrise Fund, a fund whose inception was inspired by my granddaughter Elissa's battle with leukemia when she was younger. Elissa is thankfully in remission and works with her mother, my daughter Susan, raising awareness for Childhood Cancer research through the fund. During the evening of the concert fundraiser at this beautifully restored, majestic theatre, the Glenn Miller magic could be felt all over again. The crowd's response to the orchestra and to Larry conducting was overwhelming. It was such a memorable evening for my entire family. While Larry was at the helm, he took the Glenn Miller orchestra and he infused new life and enthusiasm into the band, reviving some of the old favorites and keeping the Glenn Miller Sound alive. As one critic wrote: "A sense of swing feeling ... seems to have returned with Larry O'Brien's assumption of the leadership of the Glenn Miller Orchestra. [Larry] has steered his orchestra in the direction the Miller music followers demand, the band's basic foundation-the Glenn Miller Music."

Larry has now retired and lives with his wife in Hawaii. However, the world famous, Glenn Miller Orchestra, is the most popular and sought after big band in the world today for both concert and swing dance engagements. The present Glenn Miller Orchestra was formed in 1956 and has been touring consistently since, playing an average of 300 live dates a year all around the world. What an honor to know Larry O'Brien, I am truly humbled by his kind foreword for this book. I am so proud to know him and call him my friend, a man who created the continuing legacy of the world famous Glenn Miller Orchestra.

Larry O'Brien has always been humble about his calling saying, "What we're trying to do is run this band the way we feel Glenn would have if he were still here." Believe me Larry, Glenn would have been more than proud and honored that you have kept his music and all of his fans, "In The Mood."

Larry and the orchestra take us back to those days when Glenn was still with us. However, when you think about it, Glenn Miller will never really be gone. The words written by poet John Keats so long ago certainly apply to Glenn's music: A thing of beauty is a joy forever. Its loveliness increases. It will never pass into nothingness..."

Very rare photo from 1940 of the Glenn Miller orchestra, playing at Ebbet's Field.

October 5, 1944- meeting Bing while I was a Sgt in the Marine Corps. and he was in Oakland, California for a U.S.O. Camp Show. At 22 years of age, this was one of the greatest thrills of my life. (Jack Ellsworth, private collection)

Bing Crosby

"Unless we make Christmas an occasion to share our blessings, all the snow in Alaska won't make it 'white'."
~ Bing Crosby

    One of the greatest influences in my life and one of my favorites since I was a young boy would have to be Bing Crosby. To me, Bing had a sound and a charisma like no other. It has been said that the Crosby voice has been heard by more people than any other voice in the world and that during the 1940's, his voice was heard somewhere in the world every minute of every day. He was arguably the most famous man in the world for most of the period. He had no peer.

    Multi-talented, in addition to his superb vocalizing, Bing was an Academy Award winner. He was the consummate emcee and a great comedian (consider the Road series with Bob Hope!) He could even dance! Talk about accomplishments? According to the Guinness Book of World Records, the song "White

Christmas" sung by Bing Crosby, is the best-selling single of all time, with estimated sales in excess of 50 million copies worldwide!

The third largest selling single, his version of "Silent Night," sold over 30 million copies. His career spanned over five decades. Bing was truly in a class by himself and an inspiration to so many singers who followed, including Frank Sinatra who called Bing "The idol of my youth," Perry Como also patterned his style from Bing.

Author Ken Barnes says, [1]"It would be no empty statement to say that Bing Crosby was the most durable, the most respected and the most loved performer of this century." Ken also wrote, "It was impossible for anyone who met Bing Crosby not to be impressed by him. Most people loved him and admired him as a performer and as a person..... Certainly, he had a tendency to be enigmatic. But he was never boorish or unkind to anyone. Also, I can honestly say that I have never seen a star who was more considerate to his fans than Bing."

One of my favorite Bing Crosby stories is about the New York cab driver who commented to his famous passenger, "Has anyone ever told you that you look a lot like Bing Crosby"? "Yes," Bing replied, "I have heard that but I happen to know Bing Crosby is a much better looking man."

I first met Bing in Washington, D.C. in 1944. We were introduced through a publicity man. I remember Bing stepped off an elevator and he came over to talk to me. We stood off in a corner talking about music, his records and his career. I can still see him now, standing there. It was well known that Bing was colorblind and he often dressed in mismatched attire and yet, it somehow just added to his charm. Standing in that spot talking to one of my heroes, I remember thinking that it would forever be one of the biggest moments of my life and I was right. It still is.

Since first meeting Bing, we corresponded regularly and met on several occasions. He was always most kind and gracious. You can imagine how elated I was to have the privilege of interviewing Bing while he was appearing in New York in December of 1976. Here is the full interview conducted over the phone while I was at WLIM.

Bing Crosby Interview- December 18th 1976

BING: Hello?

JACK: Hello Bing.

BING: Yes sir, how are you Jack?

JACK: Ah, it's great to talk to you.

BING: How's things out in Long Island?
JACK: Everything is just wonderful out here. We've got a beautiful Christmas season out here and we're playing your Christmas records like crazy.

BING: That-A-Boy!

JACK: Bing, I'll tell ya, you're phenomenal. You're singing better today than ever and the reviews of your show at the Uris Theatre have just been fantastic. How do you account for that? Young fella like you singing so great?

BING: Well, they're great songs! A bunch of great songs that were provided for me by some great writers. And, people like to hear them no matter who sings them I guess... and wonderful audiences and they've been most responsive. .. and the family and myself and Rosie Clooney and Joe Bushkin are really elated at the way it's gone.

JACK: Well you know Bing, it's a great thrill for me because I'll tell ya, I've been a Bing Crosby admirer since I was just a little rascal. I heard your first records, the old Brunswick record, you know, 'Just One More Chance' and 'Learn to Croon' You've been my idol ever since I can remember and through the years, I've just been following your career as closely as possible

BING: Well, you gotta aim higher than that Jack.

JACK: Ah...gee well, what a great kick for me to be in the business now as I have been for so many years and be able to play your records so often on the air! You know we had that regular show of yours, ya know 'Bing Crosby in Hollywood' ...I wrote you about that, we got a lot of response on that.

BING: Yes!.. and you're out in? ...What town are you located in out there?

JACK: We're in Patchogue.

BING: Patchogue is a very famous old town.

JACK: Yes, have you ever been out this way?

BING: Oh, I used to play golf all over Long Island.

JACK: They've got some great courses out here.

BING: I've played them all.

JACK: Bing, we still receive a lot of requests for your records and the new ones have been so very well received, particularly like that 'Send in the Clowns.' You did a great job on that and then the thing you did with Fred Astaire.

BING: Yes, then I've got two or three more albums out. I did a Spanish American thing with Paul Smith. You know things like 'Caliente el Sol' and 'Frenesi' and things like that with English and Spanish lyrics... and then I did sort of a jazz band thing with Paul Smith and then I did, it's called 'A Southern Memoir' ..then in England I did a very good album called, 'Feels Good, Feels Right' with an orchestra in England...Oh I've done five, six albums in the last 18 months.

JACK: Bing, of all the records you've made through the years are there two or three that stand out in your mind as favorites, where you feel you did your best work?

BING: Ah yes, but it's a song you probably never heard of, from a record you never heard of, it's called 'My Isle of Golden Dreams.'

JACK: Oh I remember that. Did you do that with Lani McIntinyre?

BING: (laughs) I don't know who it was, I just like the way the voice sounded in that particular record.

JACK: Well, I think someone once said, (a collector in New York I knew by the name of Bob Weil) you also like a thing called 'Cabin in the Pines.' Remember that one?

BING: Yes, yes sure, indeed I do, great song.

JACK: Well, I guess you've done thousands of records.

BING: Yes...I don't know, (laughs) they say two or three thousand.

JACK: Bing, what are your plans, I know you're finishing up at the Uris Theatre and where do we go from here?

BING: Well, we close Sunday night then I go home for Christmas, then we do a big show in San Francisco...and then we've got, well nothing, more except American Sportsmen, that's a T.V. thing shooting quail...and then I've got a big special to be done the end of February, an hour and a half thing with a big cast ...and then we do some more concerts. I have to do one for Santa Clara University in San Jose. Just not really too much.

JACK: Well Bing, how do you figure, you're not working as much as you used to but you're still in there plugging and you sound fantastic. Now you mentioned something about the songwriters of today. Who are some of the young writers that you're impressed with especially?

BING: Oh, Carole King and the Carpenters and Neil Sedaka and Neil Diamond. There are so many of them Jack, you just couldn't enumerate them and they're all very good indeed, ..like James Taylor. Endless lists and they write such good things. It's too bad that the way some of the groups play them, you don't get the words.

JACK: That's true, yes it's unfortunate....Bing, when you were first coming up, let's go back to the days when you were at the Paramount Theater in New York, your last live stage appearance, what was that in the 20's or early 30's?

BING: No, that was early 30's but I did lots of shows in New York after that, benefits and things at the Garden and the Waldorf Astoria and the Shubert Theater... but the first time with my own show.

JACK: With your own show, I see...well Bing, in the early days back in the 30's and 40's, young people had a greater opportunity to break into show business. Through their associations with the bands....like you did with Paul Whiteman and Frank did with Tommy Dorsey. What does a young person do today... someone who feels he or she has a little talent and wants to move ahead? What route would this person take?

BING: Well, Jack, in my time there wasn't much competition when you consider that the only people singing the way I sang would be Rudy Vallee, Ozzie Nelson, Russ Columbo... only five or six fellows. Will Osborne was another... so there really wasn't too much competition. Now, the competition is fierce. I think if someone has talent, they should give it a whirl... sing as often as they can, any place.... schools, parish entertainment, wherever they can get up on their feet and sing. Sing around the house and learn poise, presence and ease and then just take a good whack at it. If it doesn't come off, drop it quickly. Don't get hooked on something that's going to be futile, you know. Drop it and get into a worthwhile activity if you find you can't make it professionally, but give it a try. Let somebody tell you whether or not you have real talent for advancement, whether you have a good feel for tempo or rhythm or for timing and reading lines or whatever. Let some expert listen to you and give you an idea. And, don't be discouraged if he tells you he doesn't think you can do it, you gave it a try. Just drop it and get into something else.

JACK: Well, you have to have the aptitude. It's like I often say to young people who want to get into the broadcasting business. I say 'We'll give you an audition and we'll tell you what we think'... and it's like you wouldn't try to make a career out of being a mechanic if you have no mechanical inclination or aptitude....

BING:...that's right.

JACK: ...and the same thing, you wouldn't want to sing if you couldn't carry a tune... and yet there are some people who struggle along for years without the tools and it is unfortunate.... Bing, you're a busy man and I don't like to take up too much of your time but do you remember the first time we met?

BING: I think you were in the Marines at Oak Knoll Hospital.

JACK: Well, that's right but before that, you were in Washington, D.C. In 1943...

BING: ..That's right, I was doing a show with Dinah Shore...

JACK: Yes, and Ben Roscoe introduced us... I met you in the lobby of the Mayflower Theater...Mayflower Hotel it was rather...

BING: That's right.

JACK: .... and it was such a great thrill for me. Well Bing, God bless you, you're beautiful and I think you're the greatest thing that ever happened to show business.

BING: Thank you Jack, I hope you have a nice holiday now!

JACK: Keep singing for another 72 years will you Bing?

BING: Okay Pal!

JACK: My best to your whole family, Thank you Bing. Bye bye.

BING: Bye, bye Jack!

My last interview with Bing was a highlight of my career and a day I will never forget. I was telling my grandchildren recently how very much Bing Crosby meant to me as not only a performer but as a role model.

I remember vividly the date, October 14, 1977. I was driving home on the Sunrise Highway on Long Island when the news came on the radio stating that Bing had died. I slowly pulled over to the side of the road. I sat there alone for a long time, sadly and gratefully reflecting about a hero of my youth, not just about the performer but the man, thinking about his kindness to me, remembering our long friendship... and I wept.

---

[1]Ken Barnes, *The Crosby Years* (New York: St Martins, 1980) (London, 1987) (London: Elm Tree Books, 1980)

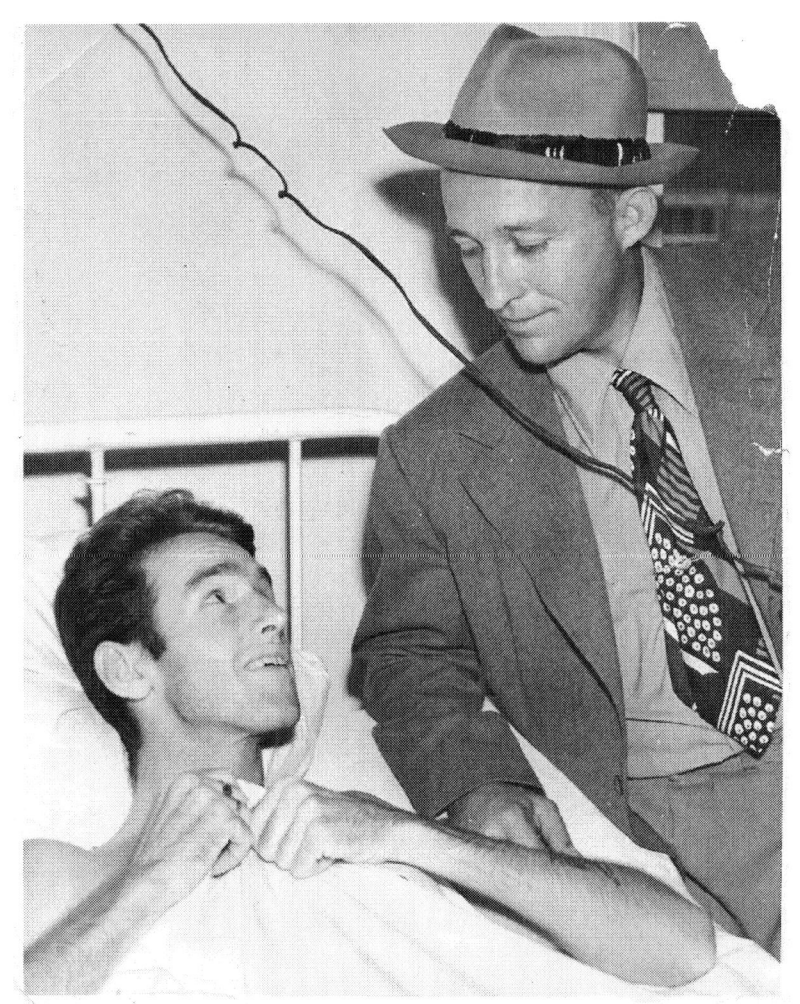

Extremely rare photo of Bing in 1944 visiting an injured soldier at Oak Knoll Naval Hospital. I had the honor of being present when this photo was taken. (Jack Ellsworth, private collection)

L-R: Jack Benny, Dick Powell, Ken Murray, Bing Crosby,
Shirley Ross and Tommy Dorsey (partially obscured) - 1948
Credit: NBC photo
(Jack Ellsworth, private collection)

Bing Crosby

August 28, 1973

Dear Jack:

Thanks for your letter. Sorry I missed seeing you up at the Rainbow Room. It was rather hectic up there - hundreds of people falling all over one another, but I still had an opportunity for a nice visit with Lucille Armstrong. She's a lovely little lady.

Delighted to hear that you've been programming my musical autobiography every week, and that you've elicited some excellent listener response.

I hope the series, "Bing In Hollywood" goes equally well.

We'll do the interview next time I'm in New York, Jack. I don't know when that's going to be, but I hope this fall or winter.

Yes, I remember Ben Roscoe, but I couldn't for the life of me tell you where he is now. I haven't heard a word of him for many years.

I'm sure that with the hustle and drive that Ben possessed, he is prospering. I hope so. Nice guy.

All best wishes, Jack -

As ever,

Bing Crosby

BC:lm
Mr. Jack Ellsworth
Island Broadcasting System
P. O. Box 230
Patchogue, Long Island, New York 11772

Bing Crosby

May 27, 1975

Dear Jack:

No, I never received your original letter written on September 24th, of which you recently sent me a copy.

Glad you liked "That's Entertainment". I think it was one of the best things that has been put together in the way of a film documentary and I imagine that MGM has enough material left in their library for two more such films.

In fact, I understand they have one underway already.

I don't know when I'll be in New York again, Jack, but I'll be glad to tape an interview with you next time I am, and I'll try and let you know well in advance —

Warmest regards,

Bing

Bing Crosby

BC:lm

Mr. Jack Ellsworth
Island Broadcasting System
P. O. Box 230
Patchogue, Long Island, New York 11772

Bing Crosby

February 13, 1976

Dear Jack:

Thanks for your letter. Glad you liked the Christmas TV Show. Of course, working with Fred always stimulates anybody who likes to try to achieve some measure of perfection.

The album that you speak about - called "That's What Life Is All About" - is being released in America in February, so I guess you'll be able to pick it up after that time.

I hope some time we can get together for an interview when I'm in the East.

If you see that I'm there, get in touch with my office and they'll put you in touch with me -

Warmest regards,

Bing Crosby

BC:lm

Mr. Jack Ellsworth
P. O. Box 230
Patchogue, Suffolk County
Long Island, New York 11772

Tommy Dorsey and I having a laugh, Providence R.I. 1948

Tommy Dorsey

"My greatest teacher was not a vocal coach, not the work of other singers, but the way Tommy Dorsey breathed and phrased on the trombone."
~Frank Sinatra

    The music I have always selected for my radio show is music form the "Golden -Era" of popular music. However, we have also been known to add some "adult standards," releases from new artists whose style best fits our format. An artist for example like Michael Bublé or Marlene VerPlanck, both artists who as beautifully written on Marlene's website, "pay loving care to the great standards and new songs from our finest composers, while ignoring mediocre pop tunes."

    Even back in the 1980's and 90's, we featured new recordings by Rosemary Clooney, , Jack Jones, Tony Bennett and such big bands as those led by Ray Anthony, Larry O'Brien, Frankie Capp, Gene Harris and Ben Grisafi.

Some years back, the NBC Show paid tribute to one of the giants in the popular music world, Tommy Dorsey. Tommy was a strong advocate of high standards in popular music. It was said that even in his lifetime, Tommy wouldn't have recorded "Doggie in the Window" for all the tea in China. However, a trite novelty song like that is mild indeed compared with some of today's so-called pop music where four letter words are the norm. Like Tommy, it is refreshing to know that many true artists and musicians still exist who maintain a moral standard in selecting quality popular music to cover.

Tommy Dorsey's widow Jane Dorsey once said that the "Sentimental Gentleman of Swing" would have taken a pretty unsentimental view of music developments since his passing. Jazz critic Richard Sudhalter quoted her as saying that Tommy hated the popular music that had all the "noise and fakery" that comes with it. He used to urge other bandleaders to keep playing, keep reaching the kids. If they didn't he used to say, the young people of today would hear nothing but trash and have to swallow it. He didn't want that for his kids or anyone else's."

Sudhalter recalled Tommy Dorsey as a true giant in the world of popular music. Known as the "Star Maker," Tommy Dorsey introduced many famous singers and musicians. Frank Sinatra came first into his own with the Dorsey Band. Other future name performers began with Dorsey. People like Jo Stafford, Connie Haines, Jack Leonard and Edythe Wright. He featured such great sidemen as Buddy Rich, Johnny Mince, Buddy DeFranco, Bunny Berigan and Ziggy Elman.

Dick Haymes, who succeeded Sinatra with Dorsey, once told me, "Tommy's band was the greatest of them all...so consistent and dependable. They might be off for for maybe twenty minutes but they'd soon be back in the groove with more of that great Dorsey sound."

We could sure use a Tommy Dorsey today. Sy Oliver, the great arranger who is responsible for such Dorsey hits as "Opus

Number One," "On the Sunny Side of the Street" and "Well Get It" once commented, "They say no man is irreplaceable. Well, I'd like to see someone replace Tommy Dorsey."

Tommy knew the three components that make music are melody, rhythm and harmony. His band could play both sweet and swing music with equal dexterity, in some ways, better than any of the other big bands.

I had the great opportunity to first meet Tommy Dorsey while working at WHIM in Providence. He was playing at a ballroom called the Rhodes on the Pawtuxet. Tommy also started his radio show on our station and I appeared with him in downtown Providence with a huge crowd at the theatre where he was performing. I then was thrilled to interview him in at the station and again the early 1950's while working at WALK.

We have Tommy Dorsey, "The Sentimental Gentleman of Swing" to thank not only for his beautifully mellow and sentimental trombone playing, but for maintaining such high standards in the big band world.

Interviewing the great Tommy Dorsey at WHIM in 1948
(Jack Ellsworth- private collection)

Lunch with the "Sentimental Gentleman of Swing"
Photo Credit: Walter Butterfield
(Jack Ellsworth- private collection)

To kick off Tommy's very own radio show in Providence . We appeared with him in front of the RKO Albee Theatre in Providence. What a turn out! I am just to the right of Tommy in the center

In the studio at WHIM, Providence, Rhode Island

Ella Fitzgerald - Indisputably one of the greatest female vocalists of all time!

Ella Fitzgerald

"It isn't where you came from, it's where you're going that counts." ~ Ella Fitzgerald

Ella Fitzgerald was originally called "The First Lady of Swing" when she was just a teenage vocalist with Chick Webb's band. Soon thereafter and forevermore she was known as "The First Lady of Song."

In a career that spanned nearly sixty years Ella won many polls, awards and accolades, the most prestigious of which was as a 1979 Kennedy Center honoree along with Aaron Copland, Henry Fonda and Martha Graham.

Among her many distinguished admirers were Duke Ellington, Count Basie, Louis Armstrong, Benny Goodman and countless other singers, composers and musicians. I think Bing Crosby said it most accurately, "Man, woman or child, Ella is the best." Ira Gershwin once remarked, "I never knew how good our songs were until Ella Fitzgerald sang them."

Among her best recordings is the George and Ira Gershwin songbook recorded with Nelson Riddle and his orchestra. There are many other Fitzgerald collections of famous composers and their best songs including songbooks of music by Jerome Kern, Harold Arlen, Irving Berlin, Johnny Mercer, Cole Porter and Rodgers and Hart.

I remember hearing Ella when she first began her career. As a lifelong admirer of Benny Goodman, I was delighted with the three recordings she made with Benny in 1936. Ella was under contract to another record company and there were some legal problems which resulted in the temporary withdrawal of those sides. Happily, they have been reissued. Benny, always appreciative of great talent, was one of the first to recognize Ella's potential. It is especially significant since Benny was seldom enthralled with vocalists, concentrating more on side men.

For me Ella has always been a total joy. She made us aware of so many songs that might otherwise have been ignored. Consider the Jerome-Kern-Dorothy Fields gem "Remind Me" from the Kern songbook. Once she began to sing, it was always captivating. Ella once said about herself, "I'm very shy, and I shy away from people but the moment I hit the stage, it's a different feeling. I get nerve from somewhere; maybe it's because it's something I love to do."

Whether she sang about happy or unrequited love, she conveyed a certain warmth, charm and sweetness. I always felt that Ella never lost that little girl appeal of her "Tisket-A-Tasket" days. I am reminded of a reference to the poet Shelley who once described, "Forever the enchanted child, born into a world so un-childlike."

Ella was totally unique in her uncanny ability to deliver a song, often giving one new insight into the words and music. She could take the word "love" and make it sound like it had four syllables and it never seemed forced or unnatural.

Not many people know that in 1937 Ella recorded a follow-up to Tisket-A-Tasket" called "I Found My Yellow Basket." It never received much attention probably because the original couldn't be topped. One thing is certain, we'll never find another Ella but thank God for all of her definitive versions of countless classic American Standards. They are constant reminders of how good popular singing can be.

Lady Ella lost her yellow basket in 1936....and in 1996 we lost her. She may be gone physically but her legacy of magnificent song will live on.

Fred Astaire and his inimitable style.

Fred Astaire

"Do it big, do it right and do it with style."
~ Fred Astaire

When you talk about the greatest stars of the 20th century, without question the name "Fred Astaire" is at the top of the list. It has been said that his signature style of dancing with its inimitable finesse, coupled with his gentle demeanor, has delighted every generation.

Over his long film career, Fred had many talented and beautiful dance partners such as Ginger Rogers, Cyd Charisse, Rita Hayworth, Eleanor Powell and many others. His wonderful disposition and reputation preceded him. Cyd Charisse once said, "When you worked with him he was a gentleman and in private he was a gentleman." In public he was a very humble, sweet man, a marvelous person.

I remember seeing Fred in films many times over. My favorites still are, "Swing Time," "Top Hat" and "Follow the Fleet."

Fred had a lighter than air constitution. His half-spoken singing was always delightful. His dancing was brilliantly inventive. Gene Kelly once observed, "Fred would give the audience pleasure just walking across the floor." Fred himself once remarked, "I suppose I made it look easy but gee why did I work and worry? I have no desire to prove anything by dancing. I have never used it as a outlet or as a means of expressing myself. I just dance. I just put my feet in the air and I move them around."

In 1953, I remember reading an article about a set of recordings Fred made of songs from his films. I was anxious to obtain copies of the recordings so I wrote Fred a letter asking him about its release. Imagine my surprise when I received a hand-written reply on his own personal stationery.

Fred kindly and generously took the time to give me details of the much anticipated and now classic record set, "The Astaire Story." As Fred mentioned in his note, the album was conceived of and produced by Norman Granz. The song selections give an overview of Astaire's singing career. As Fred also mentioned in his letter to me, there are "impromptu dance noises" as he demonstrates his tap dancing on a few tracks.

Producer Norman Granz had this to say about Fred, "For years, I've had a great admiration for Mr. Astaire and so, I feel, have a few million other people. I'm not sure it was only his dancing and singing; perhaps it was his clothes or the way he wore them; or maybe it was the way he walked. (As a matter of fact, I don't even like to call him a dancer; I really believe that he is basically a graceful walker. And his grace is that God-given kind that transcends ordinary hoofing.) But whatever it was, there was something about Mr. Astaire that made him everybody's boy."

I so agree with Norman Granz. How can you not love Fred Astaire? Many dancers have come and gone since Fred Astaire's feet have graced the dance floor. Mr. Astaire will always be above them all, his magic and grace forever unmatched.

How true it was said of him that he, "was both fragility and steel." Toward the end of his life, Fred remarked, "Oh, I hope God gives me one more year." We lost Fred in June of 1987. We are not only grateful that God gave him that one more year, we are forever grateful that God gave us Fred Astaire.

Hand written letter from Fred Astaire (pages 210-211)

"My dear Mr. Ellsworth, Thank you for your letter. The "long playing record" referred to in the clipping you enclosed is really an album of 8 sides (LP) consisting of 3 vocals + six instrumentals (5 with impromptus dance noises).
It is coming out on the Mercury label – a project of Norman Granz and his Jazz at the Philharmonic group.
Would advise you to write to him for further details as to release etc.
Hope the thing interests you. It was great fun to make.
Kindest Regards, Fred Astaire"

Thursday

Fred Astaire

MEMO

My dear Mr. Ellsworth:—

Thank you for your letter. The "long playing record" referred to in the clipping you enclosed is really an album of 8 sides (L.P.) consisting of 32 vocals + six instrumentals (5 with impromptu dance noises).

It is coming out on the Mercury label — a project

Fred Astaire

MEMO

of Norman Granz + his Jazz at The Philharmonic group. Would advise you to write to him for further details as to release etc.

Hope this thing interests you — it was great fun to make.

Kindest regards —

Fred Astaire

The gifted and prolific writer and lyricist, P.G. Wodehouse who was part author and writer of 15 plays and of 250 lyrics for some 30 musical comedies, many of them produced in collaboration with Jerome Kern and Guy Bolton.

P.G. Wodehouse

"I know I was writing stories when I was five. I don't know what I did before that. Just loafed I suppose."
~ P. G. Wodehouse

It was on a lovely spring afternoon in 1970 that I had the thrill of interviewing Mr. P.G.Wodehouse. We sat on his comfortable sun porch at his home in Remsenburg, N.Y.. Mr. Wodehouse enjoyed a long and illustrious career in music and literature. His contributions to the world of popular music included collaborations with Jerome Kern, Guy Bolton and Oscar Hammerstein. Mr. Wodehouse first worked with Jerome Kern in London, England in 1906. They wrote several songs together and later collaborated on various other shows including "Miss Springtime", an early Zeigfeld show, and one called "Have a Heart" which ran for five years in New York and then on the road. After that came "Oh Boy" in 1917, a show which was an enormous success.

Among the songs in "Oh Boy" were "Nesting Time in Flatbush", "A Pal Like You", "An Old Fashioned Wife" and the most memorable, "Til The Clouds Roll By". Another great success that same year was "Leave It To Jane". Again Jerome Kern wrote all the music and P.G. Wodehouse did the lyrics. "Leave It To Jane" enjoyed a three year off Broadway revival in the mid fifties. Mr. Wodehouse said he really loved that show.

I asked Mr. Wodehouse, "Of all the songs you wrote with Kern, which were your favorites?" He replied, "well I'm very fond of "The Sirens Song" from "Leave It To Jane, and, of course, "Bill" which is in "Show Boat." We originally wrote "Bill" for an earlier show called "Oh Lady, Lady." That was about 1918. It was a farce starring Vivienne Segal, but Jerry felt "Bill" was too slow so the song lay dormant, so to speak, for about eight years. In 1927, while I was out in Hollywood, Jerry came to me one day and asked if he could use "Bill" for "Show Boat"... and I said, "Oh yes, of course you can..." and it was a big success. I must say that of all the Jerry Kern melodies, "Bill" is my special favorite. Of course, all of his stuff was so good.

I asked Mr. Wodehouse "What kind of a man was Jerome Kern? You worked with him so often and knew him very well." "He was a very delightful fellow, very cheerful and full of pep. We got along awfully well. He was such a splendid fellow to work with. He used to work practically all night. Once while he was living in Bronxville, he called at 3:00 A.M. and woke me up to say, I've got the melody for the second act number; and then he played it for me over the phone. Then I wrote a dummy of it and then did the lyrics. Then he continued to work all night. I think that's what killed him. He wasn't strong at all.. not an awfully strong fellow and he never wanted to go to bed."

I asked Mr. Wodehouse if Kern was ever concerned about competition with other composers. "Not while I knew him. He was absolutely leading the field in those days. Then a little later George Gershwin became known. George was actually a protégé of Jerry's and if Jerry needed help on a show, he'd get George to assist him with the music. Later Richard Rodgers came along. I understand toward the end of his life Jerry was fairly gloomy about the younger generation knocking at the door. He was very sensitive about his position. He fretted if he couldn't sort of be the leader."

I told Mr. Wodehouse that one of Kern's loveliest songs was "I've Told Every Little Star" from 'Music in the Air.' Bing Crosby said it was his favorite and that the melody was inspired by the song of a finch singing outside his window one morning while he was vacationing in Quogue. NY I then whistled what could have been the bird's song. Mr. Wodehouse chuckled, "That's a delightful story, isn't it?" I then said, "I've been told that much of Jerome Kern's music was inspired by German folk songs. Is that true?" "I believe it was. I'm not sure but I think "Till The Clouds Roll By" was taken from a German folk melody--or based on one. The great thing about Jerry in those days was that he was so high spirited and he'd do the light numbers so very well. When we worked together Jerry generally wrote the music first, but if it was a comic song, then I did the lyrics first. But generally he'd do the music first and I'd fit the lyrics to it. I always preferred writing that way. I was awfully inclined to make a thing just like a set of light verse... you know too regular a meter. I remember a song in "Oh Boy", the chorus ran something like this... if every day you give her diamonds and pearls on a string... well I never would have thought of that. I mean the first beat came... if you give her diamonds and pearls on a string... to me it wouldn't have scanned properly. I mean my stuff when I wrote the lyrics first was always much too regular."

I asked Mr. Wodehouse what he thought about the then current musical "My Fair Lady"? He said, "That is such a wonderful show. The music was awfully good by Lerner & Loewe." He said he didn't care for Rock and Roll and Country music. His comment was, "Well I don't like it myself, but that may just be an old fashioned point of view. But before I forget, I haven't seen "Hello Dolly" as yet, but I understand the big number is a world beater."

I then asked Mr. Wodehouse about his present activities. Perhaps best known to many for his writing, particularly about the character "Jeeves," he said... I just finished a novel yesterday. It needs a little more work. My great trouble these days is getting a thing long enough. Publishers want 70,000 words and I'm very apt to write about 63,000 so I have to do a bit of lengthening.

I then asked about a movie he worked on. "In 1937 there was a Fred Astaire movie called "A Damsel in Distress." Wasn't that based on your book?" "Yes, I worked on that production. You'll remember Ginger Rogers stepped aside for that film. She wanted to do more dramatic roles, so Fred's leading lady was Joan Fontaine. Fred had to work with her on the dancing because she wasn't quite up to Ginger's talents, but she was a delightful, lovely leading lady. The Gershwins wrote the music for "A Damsel in Distress" and there were some wonderful songs that have endured very well indeed. There was "Nice Work If You Can Get It," and "A Foggy Day."

"Well Mr. Wodehouse," I said, "this has been a very rewarding experience for me! I've wanted to meet you ever since my dear old dad introduced me to your work. He was a great admirer of Bolton, Wodehouse and Kern. And I hear that guy Bolton lives in this area and that you fellows still get together." "Yes indeed," Mr. Wodehouse replied. "He remains a very close friend. We worked awfully well together on over twenty shows." I replied "If only Jerome Kern were alive you could do another show." Mr. Wodehouse nodded and said, "Oh Yes!"

"In closing, I questioned Mr. Wodehouse, "What advice would you give to young people who were interested in writing for the theatre or perhaps writing books and stories such as you have written?" "Well," he answered, "that's rather difficult. I'm very glad I'm not starting writing today because the market has practically disappeared. In the early days when I was living in Greenwich Village and trying to earn a living by writing, there were all those pulp magazines like Argosy, The Blue Book, The Peoples and dozens of them. If you wrote a story you could always land it somewhere ... and get about fifty dollars for it. Even the slick paper magazines, they've all disappeared. Colliers is gone, the American Magazine, The Delineator and so many others. Getting a story published today isn't easy."

After chatting briefly, our interview ended and I departed saying I hoped we'd meet again soon... unfortunately, we never did. I was so fortunate to have spent an afternoon with this legend, a man whose work will live on forever.

The great Frank Sinatra, early 1940's

Frank Sinatra

Whatever else has been said about me personally is unimportant. When I sing, I believe. I'm honest.

~ Frank Sinatra

Frank Sinatra, a magic name in the entertainment world for as long as any of us can remember. It's been fourteen years since we lost Frank. When the world received the news in 1998 that Frank Sinatra had died, we didn't want to believe it. We wanted him to go on forever. A world without Frank Sinatra? Impossible! From the earliest days with Harry James, Tommy Dorsey and at the New York Paramount, he has always been there, as a part of our lives. And oh, those songs: "I'll Never Smile Again," "Night and Day," "Nancy with the Laughing Face," "I've Got You Under My Skin," "It Was a Very Good Year" and we will never be able to hold back the tears when we hear his closing theme, "Put Your Dreams Away."

In 1943, while I was in the U.S. Marine Corps, stationed at Pearl Harbor, my fellow Marines and I used to listen to Frank's Hit Parade broadcast via short wave radio. One of my buddies was

Mickey McElroy from North Bergen, New Jersey. He was an ardent Sinatra fan, When Frank would come on the air he would call it "S Hour." We all agreed that the first one of our group who got back to the states would contact Frank and let him know how much we enjoyed his broadcast while we were overseas.

I was lucky to return first and was subsequently stationed near Los Angeles. While on liberty, I went to the CBS studio in Hollywood where the Hit Parade originated. I went backstage and asked to see Frank. He came out to greet me and was delighted when I told him about "S Hour!" He called to his manager, George Evans, "Hey George! These guys really listen to our broadcasts out in the Pacific!" Frank seemed really thrilled.

One of the highlights of my career was sitting in on one of Frank's recording sessions and also conducting an interview with him. In 1949, I contacted Mani Sacks, a Columbia records executive and a close friend of Frank's. He very kindly invited me to a Sunday afternoon recording session. He also set up the interview for the same afternoon.

I asked my younger sister Ruth to accompany me. She excitedly accepted. When we arrived at the recording studio, there was no one else there. There was no audience. There I was with Ruth, the orchestra, the arranger, the sound technicians and Frank! What a once in a lifetime experience! During the recording session, Frank sang, "Don't Cry Joe," "It All Depends on You" and "If I Ever Love Again," and "Bye, Bye Baby." I was very impressed with how closely Frank worked with the orchestra leader Hugo Winterhalter and with Sy Oliver, the famous arranger and friend from the Tommy Dorsey days. There was a strong atmosphere of professionalism and respect. It was so interesting to watch their reactions during playbacks. Tenor sax player Al Klink, long featured with the legendary Glenn Miller orchestra, also played in various orchestras who recorded with Sinatra. Al once told me how much he admired Frank. He said if something goes wrong during a record session, Frank always takes the blame. He never criticizes any of the musicians.

After the session, it was time for our interview. Frank seemed tired after long hours of recording. At the beginning, he didn't seem overjoyed at the prospect of doing an interview with some DJ that he hardly knew. However, during the interview, Frank became aware that I was very familiar with his career and he began to respond most cordially.

In the interview, Frank said how he disliked most of the popular songs of the day. He went on to explain that many of them sound like they were written between breakfast and lunch on a streetcar. One of the songs he spoke of was, "Toolie, Oolie, Doolie." Frank remarked, "Back in my days with Tommy Dorsey, we recorded many great songs but it's been downhill ever since." He went on to say, "I wish the songwriters would get together and write some good material instead of "Lavender Blue" and "Woody Woodpecker."

Frank explained, "I think they say that an artist is as good as his material and in nine out of ten cases that holds true--very true. With a good song going for you, you almost can't miss. We've had a smattering of amateur songwriters and I don't feel amateur songs belong in the professional music business. Until a songwriter has proven that he can write a hit at least three times a year--, well then I don't think those songs should be done in the professional music business because they hurt the artist and the performed and orchestras. Again I think back to the days when I was with Tommy. In that era he had such a great band with a lot going with it. There were so many fine songs. We had tremendous tunes in those days. I'll never forget working with Tommy Dorsey's arranger geniuses such as Axel Stordahl, Sy Oliver, Paul Weston, Dean Kincaide, etc. With talent like that going for you, plus such great songs, plus the Pied Pipers, why a Myna bird could come up with a hit platter. Yes, Tommy Dorsey was the General Motors of the band business."

I think it is quite evident that Frank has always been deeply concerned about the meaning of the songs he has sung. Not all singers show such concern.

As the interview drew to a close, I thanked Frank for his time and interest in our interview. Frank kindly remarked as I was leaving, "Jack, it was great having you with me in the studio today and I want to thank you for your continued support of my career.

I also look forward to the release dates of our interview." As I walked out of the studio that day, I fully realized what an amazing experience I had just had. I knew that it was an occasion that I would long remember.

As the technology in 1949 was limited, I recorded Frank's interview with a microphone on a reel-to-reel recorder. It was later transferred to an acetate disc. I was later thrilled, as were my listeners, to share the interview on my Memories in Melody show on WGSM in Huntington, New York.

In the years to follow, Frank continued to thrill audiences with his distinctive sound, music and memorable film roles. Even in the 1970's Frank was playing to sold out crowds. Whenever I had the good fortune of being honored by my peers, by our radio station WLIM, by WALK radio or by local dignitaries, Frank always acknowledged my presence and accomplishments with a hand signed photograph or personal letter.

Back in the mid-80's I notified Frank that he had won our popularity contest as favorite male vocalist. He responded in a taped message;

> "Hey, I wanna tell you I was thrilled and delighted when my old friend, Jack Ellsworth, called to tell me that WLIM had selected me as the all-time favorite male vocalist. That certainly is a great honor to me - and I mean that too. And congratulations to WLIM for programming such fine music all day, every day. Be sure to stay tuned to WLIM at 1580 on your dial for Long Island's best listening. And thanks to you, the WLIM listeners, for all you votes. It means a lot to me and I want you to know how much I appreciate it."

Shortly thereafter when I notified Frank that we were devoting a full day to his music he replied with a taped message,

> "What a kick to be honored with an entire day of my records on WLIM! I'm very grateful to Jack Ellsworth and all the guys at WLIM for devoting this day to your truly. A

full day of Sinatra is kinda heavy for me, but I want to thank all your listeners who made it possible."

Frank always encouraged listening to our station, when we had WLIM. I have another tape we played on the air where he says,

"Whenever I'm out on Long Island like visiting Jones Beach, I try to catch Jack's show. They tell me Jack even slips in a Sinatra record now and then. I'm so glad Jack now has his own radio station, WLIM and it's great to know that "Songs by Sinatra" is still heard every Sunday morning at nine. Jack has a great collection and it makes me realize just how many records I've made going back to the Harry James, Tommy Dorsey days."

Every January we presented a full day of Sinatra songs so there was something all of our listeners can look forward to. One of my favorite stories is one Frank tells on himself. I'm a bit vague on the date of this incident, but I believe it's from the early sixties.

Frank had a date with a network executive and when he arrived a bit early the receptionist advised Frank to go into the control room where his executive friend in the adjacent studio would see him through the soundproof glass. When Frank did so, his friend saw him and gave Frank the "ten minutes more" signal. Frank nodded and then turned to look at the engineer hunched over the control board. Apparently he was taping something from the studio where Frank assumed sort of audition was underway. At this point, I think it appropriate to mention that radio engineers come from a different place apart from talent who they often fail to fully appreciate. Their concern is for the technical end of broadcasting and little else. Leaning closer to the engineer Frank remarked, say, don't I know you? Weren't you the engineer for the Tommy Dorsey Hotel broadcast remotes?" Looking over his shoulder the engineer replied, "yeah, that's right.... Singer, ain't cha?"

One more early recollection - We know that Frank did not graduate from high school and one of his classmates, the late Danny Quatrochi, a sax player from Bellport, New York, once told me that Frank wasn't a very enthusiastic student in grade school either. Danny recalled that Frank didn't like shop class and devised a method of leaving the room unnoticed. He would sit at the rear of the room near the door and before class began, Frank would insert one piece of balsa wood on the floor between the door and the frame. Then when the teacher wasn't looking, he would slip out of the room as the door closed silently against the soft wood.

Danny also said that if Frank didn't like his report card he would take a blank card from the supply closet, fill in his higher grades and take that one home to be signed. Danny said he could never figure out how Frank got the real card signed by a parent.

Back in the sixties Danny was walking along Fifth Avenue in New York City and he saw Frank coming out of a building. He ran over to greet him, but was blocked by Frank's bodyguards. Recognizing his old friend, Frank exclaimed, "OK, wait. It's my old pal Danny!" "Whereupon they embraced warmly. Proof that as they say Frank never forgets a friend. He certainly remembered me over the years and it always touched me.

Years ago Frank sent me another very special taped message to use on WLIM. He said,

> "Hello dere! This is Francis Albert. You know something? Jack Ellsworth presented his first
> program, "SONGS BY SINATRA" in 1947 - and I was only six years old. I'm so happy that
> he's still playing my music. Thank you very much, Jack!"

Today, I understand that a whole new generation of young people is embracing his music. While he is no longer with us, the music of the legendary Frank Sinatra continues to bring joy to millions. The greatest tribute I can pay to the man who took the time to support my career as much as I supported his, is to play his music on the air. My radio show "Sunday with Sinatra" has indeed been on the air since 1947 and is the longest running Sinatra radio show in the world.

It is a tribute that I am more than honored to give Frank and one that he will always deserve.

Frank performing for the American Troops during World War II in Italy, 1944. (Jack Ellsworth private collection)

Very rare photo of Frank given to me by a friend. The photo is from the mid 1940's and has never been seen or published before. (Jack Ellsworth private collection)

Telegram from Frank in 1977, when I celebrated my 25th anniversary in radio, which reads: "Dear Jack, Can it be 25 years already? How it does fly by when you're having fun. Keep up the fine work and in 25 years, I'll send you another telegram. Best Regards, Frank Sinatra"

Frank in the mid 60's in the recording studio.

Inscription: "To Jack, Many thanks for your continued support of my music – All the Best to you- Frank Sinatra '90"

Frank Sinatra

March 23, 1993

Dear Jack,

We've followed the same path for more than 45 years and, for me, it has been a joy singing and interpreting wonderful classic American music. I thank you for bringing my music to listeners throughout Long Island.

Let's keep doing it for another 45!

Best regards,

Frank Sinatra

Mr. Jack Ellsworth
WLIM Radio
Long Island Music
Woodside Avenue
Patchogue, New York 11772

Frank Sinatra

April 15, 1997

Dear Jack,

We've traveled many musical miles together, my friend. I am delighted to send cheers and bravos to you on 50 marvelous years of championing our kind of music.

As I raise a glass of bubbly, I thank you for your generous support of my career -- you're a good man!

Frank Sinatra

Mr. Jack Ellsworth
WLIM Radio
Woodside Avenue
Patchogue, N.Y. 11772

COUNT BASIE

The great band leader Count Basie.
Inscription: "To Jack, Thanx, from Count Basie"

Count Basie

"All I wanted was to be big, to be in show business and to travel... and that's what I've been doing all my life." ~ Count Basie

Many people have asked me if I have a favorite big band. That's a tough question. My top three favorites are Benny Goodman, Count Basie and Glenn Miller. Count Basie gets a special nod for consistency during half a century. He started his first band in 1935 and he remained active until the mid eighties. Basie's last recordings were released posthumously in 1986 having been recorded in 1983.

His long time producer Norman Granz said, "Basie's output has varied over his career from goodish to utterly brilliant. It is not possible to find any recorded performance by any of his groups that doesn't swing. Count Basie was a soft spoken man with an insatiable appetite for music and especially for the blues which lay at the core of all he did."

Count Basie was a genius at leading both big bands and small combos. As Norman Granz said, "He was one of the very few players whose wit at the keyboard could actually make you laugh. We can be sure that there will never be another remotely like him. May his legacy, the thousands of recordings, continue to enlighten generations still unborn who one day will want to know what a big band should sound like."

I am fortunate to have heard the Basie band in person here on Long Island on half a dozen occasions. The band appeared at Brookhaven National Laboratory, Colonie Hill, Canoe Place Inn, The Huntington House, Patchogue Medford High School and we booked him for a Skills Unlimited benefit at the Patchogue Knights of Columbus Hall.

My most memorable experience with Count Basie was at the aforementioned benefit. As the band was packing their instruments at the end of the affair, I walked over to the Count and thanked him for a magnificent performance. I shook his hand and said, "Bill, you guys are just the greatest!" He smiled and said, "I want to thank you Jack for playing our music on your radio station." I told him it was my great pleasure and that we would always play his music. As I turned to walk away, he called me back and said, "You're not hearing me, Jack! I want you to know how very much we appreciate what you do for us. Playing our music so often on your station means a lot." I was really moved and taken aback. Here was the great Count Basie making sure I knew how he felt about our love and support of his music. I'll never forget his words.

Earlier that evening between sets, I told the Count how much I enjoyed his recordings with Frank Sinatra, Billy Eckstine, Sara Vaughan, Ella Fitzgerald, Kay Starr, Joe Williams and other great singing stars. He responded by asking me, "You like listening? I can't tell you what a joy it was to work with them all. It was an honor and a great kick."

Basie's big band was known for a deceptively simple repertoire of head arrangements, combining singing riffs with strong soloists. Some of the best side men with his band over the years included Lester Young, Harry "Sweets" Edison, Eddie "Lockjaw" Davis, Grover Mitchell (who went on to lead the Count Basie Orchestra) and also Frank Wess, Frank Foster, Joe Newman, Al Grey, Buck Clayton, Dicky Wells and Vic Dickenson. It has been said that Basie, guitarist Freddy Greene, Walter Page and Jo Jones were the definitive rhythm section of the big band era.

Basie always believed that a great drummer was an important key to the swinging sound he was famous for. Among his best drummers were Gus Johnson, Harold Jones, Don Lamond, Buddy Rich, "Butch" Miles, and my favorite, Sonny Payne who rated his performance each evening on a scale of one to ten. When the band was appearing in Huntington, NY in the sixties for the Italian American Club, Sonny was sparkling. I asked him how he rated himself on this particular evening. Tossing his drumsticks in the air and deftly grabbing them, he grinned and said, "Oh, I guess about a six." I would have said "a ten" because the band was really moving at its best!

A few words should be said about Basie's great arrangers. Among the best were Neil Hefti, Bill Holman, Frank Foster, Quincy Jones, Ernie Wilkins, Billy Byers and Sammy Nestico.

As for my favorite Basie recordings, offhand I can think of almost half a dozen, "One O'clock Jump," "Blues in Hoss Flat," "I'm Shouting Again," "The Kid From Red Bank," and "The Kansas City Suite."

I could easily identify with Norman Granz who spoke these words when we lost the Count in 1984, "It is difficult for me to accept that never again will I be able to work with this great and lovable man and have the joy of listening to him play."

Thanks to the Count's many wonderful recordings, we will always be able to enjoy and share with our listeners the thrilling sounds of the greatest swing band of them all and that will continue as long as we are on the air. In fact, as many of our listeners know, for a long time I have established a tradition of opening every one of my shows with a Count Basie selection. Before I announce the date, say good morning or even officially introduce the show, I start with a swinging Basie number. I'm sure the Count would be beyond pleased to know that more than 35 years later since our conversation... I have still kept my promise.

Yours truly with my wife Dot and Count Basie at the Knights of Columbus Hall - Patchogue, New York - July 8, 1972.
Jim Mooney Photo

Cover of Percy Faith's classic Christmas album

Christmas Music and Memories

"I will honor Christmas in my heart, and try to keep it all the year." ~ Charles Dickens

In the song, "Christmas Mem'ries," Frank Sinatra sings, "Christmas Mem'ries are the sweetest ones I know." The final line of this lovely song by Marilyn Bergman and Don Costa says ... "funny, but come December I remember every Christmas I've ever known."

I doubt if any of us can remember every Christmas but I certainly have fond memories of Christmas as a boy. My dad dearly loved Christmas and all of the traditions. He made sure it was a very special time for my brother, my sister and me.

Early in December, dad brought home Christmas editions of such famous English magazines as "The Illustrated London News" and "Punch." These colorful holiday issues were filled with Dickensian scenes and enchanting Christmas stories. My dear grandmother, "Grammy" made sure we kids could enjoy Christmas shopping. All year long, she saved pennies in brown paper wrappers and presented each of us with a generous supply. There was a drug store near her home on the corner of Argyle and Cortelyou Roads. Here we could buy gifts of various inexpensive toiletries for our mother and dad, our grandparents and a few other special people. Later, when we had allowances, we shopped at Woolworths on Avenue J. When mom went on shopping trips in downtown Brooklyn, I often accompanied her on visits to A & S, Loesers, and Namms department stores. Unlike today, Christmas decorations didn't greet us until after Thanksgiving.

Christmas Eve in our home always featured a light supper and included egg nog and apple cider. We went to bed and managed to fall asleep waking at the crack of dawn. After dad stoked the furnace and the house warmed up a bit, we were led slowly downstairs with our eyes closed. Then, as we entered the living room, we had the first look at the magnificent Christmas tree. Dad always got the largest tree he could find. While we were asleep, that big pine was brought in from the garage and beautifully decorated with tinsel, old fashioned ornaments and twinkling lights. We were told that this had all been done by Santa who had also left stockings filled to the top and many gifts under the tree. For years, I never doubted the existence of Santa Claus but always wondered how he got my Iver-Johnson 28" wheel bicycle down the chimney!

One Christmas Eve, we stayed at our Gram's house and I swore I heard reindeer hooves on the roof outside my window. I even thought I saw the reflection of a sleigh on the window pane!

Christmas Day featured a roast goose and all the trimmings. Mom always made sure I had my favorite plum pudding with hard sauce while other family members enjoyed her apple and mince pies. Grammy baked delicious cookies with a dollop of her homemade jelly in the middle. Today, my wife Dot uses the same recipes much to the delight of the children, grandchildren and the whole family.

Even today, Christmas at home with the family, is still the very the best time of the year. I have been very blessed to have a wife and family who love Christmas as much as my parents and grandparents did.

My wife Dot – who is known as "Grammy," to our nine grandchildren, (as was my Grammy so many years ago) has seen to it that our kids and their little ones have been caught up in the magic of this special time even as I was back in the thirties and forties.

Dot is the most enthusiastic shopper and home decorator I have ever known. She has the knack of finding just the right gift for everyone on her ever-growing list. Dot has always worked closely with Santa in filling stockings for every child and grandchild. Our daughter Susan and our sons, Gary and Glenn found stockings on the mantle even into their thirties, and now their children have the same thrill. Dot saves for months to be sure the presents under the tree fulfill the fondest wishes of all. The only treat the family looks forward to more is an annual Christmas visit from my sister Ruth with whom I have spent every Christmas for over 80 years!

Our outdoor decorations include an old-fashioned sleigh complete with "Rudolph" and filled with a load of colorful make-believe gifts. The gazebo next to our driveway is wrapped in garland with red bows and gold bells. The front door is carefully tended to by Dot with a magnificent wreath and matching swags on either side.

Inside, we are so proud of the magnificent imported Hummel creche atop the hutch in the dining room. With tender loving care, Dot sets this up Thanksgiving week to herald in the Christmas season. This nativity is a family treasure ordered from Germany many years ago, reminding us that Christmas celebrates the birth of Jesus, our Savior.

Elsewhere through the house there are numerous elves, carolers, sprigs of holly and a lighted winter scene on the mantle piece. Below on the hearth are Mrs. Santa Claus and a Santa figure with a lapful of Christmas cards. Mistletoe hangs over the archway between the living room and the dining room.

Needless to say our live tree is a joy to behold with carefully preserved ornaments, including a few that go back over 100 years.

What would music be for any of us without the glorious music of the season? The familiar songs of Nat King Cole, Bing Crosby and Frank Sinatra have always filled our home throughout the month of December. One of my favorite Christmas songs is one Bing sings: "The Secret of Christmas is not the things you do at Christmastime but the Christmas things you do all year through." The Ray Conniff Singers put it this way: "The real meaning of Christmas is the giving of love everyday."A few other special favorites include Perry Como and Percy Faith.

Perry Como's Christmas albums are among the best. Perry was famous for his love of Christmas, especially with his extremely close family. He had a great affection for one particular holiday song, 'There is no Christmas like a Home Christmas." He recorded it first in 1950 and again nearly 20 years later. Written by an old friend, Mikey J Addy and his partner Carl Sigman, the song surely "hits home." One of my wife Dot's favorite Christmas songs recorded by Perry is "I Wish It Could Be Christmas Forever," and don't we all.

Perry's appeal spanned many generations and he was greatly respected for both his professional standards and even the standards of personal conduct that he upheld in his personal life.

In the official RCA Records memorial, his life was summed up in these few words: "50 years of music and a life well lived."

Percy Faith's "Christmas Is" is a magnificent interpretation of holiday favorites. It is one of our family's all-time Christmas favorites. Our daughter Susan and her closest friend since childhood, Lori Curiale Bridgwood love "Christmas Is" so much that they start listening to the album in October. Percy also has other glorious Christmas collections with his signature sweeping and dramatic orchestral arrangements of traditional carols.

Many do not know that Percy Faith was a child piano prodigy, but his hands were burned in a fire when he was only 18 years old. He switched to conducting and arranging. He developed a unique orchestral 'sound', with a strong emphasis on creative string work. His signature style soon became familiar to listeners everywhere. One of my favorite (non-Christmas) songs is a "Theme from 'A Summer Place'" (1960). Greats like Johnny Mathis, Doris Day and Tony Bennett all considered Percy Faith among their favorite accompanists.

I was very honored to receive letters from both Percy and Perry thanking me for my support of their music, especially during the holiday season. I hope that by continuing to play their beautiful and inspiring Christmas albums each year, I am not only keeping the traditions alive for my family, but it is my way of saying thank you for making Christmas so special.

We are also so thankful as well for our many devoted listeners and how they have expressed their appreciation over the years for our devotion to playing quality Christmas music on the air, from carols to standards. As our six year old grandson, Michael, (now twenty-two!) used to say on a message taped just for our listeners...

"God Bless Us Everyone!"

Percy Faith conducting

COLUMBIA RECORDS

A Division of Columbia Broadcasting System, Inc.

799 SEVENTH AVENUE, NEW YORK 19, NEW YORK · CIRCLE 5-7800

PERCY FAITH
Musical Director

January 10, 1957

Dear Jack:

  Please accept my sincere thanks for the tremendous amount of performances you have been giving my records. I am going to do my best to drop in and extend these thanks personally.

          Kindest regards,

          PERCY FAITH

PF:lw

Mr. Jack Elsworth
Station WALK
Patchogue, L.I., N.Y.

Letter from Percy Faith

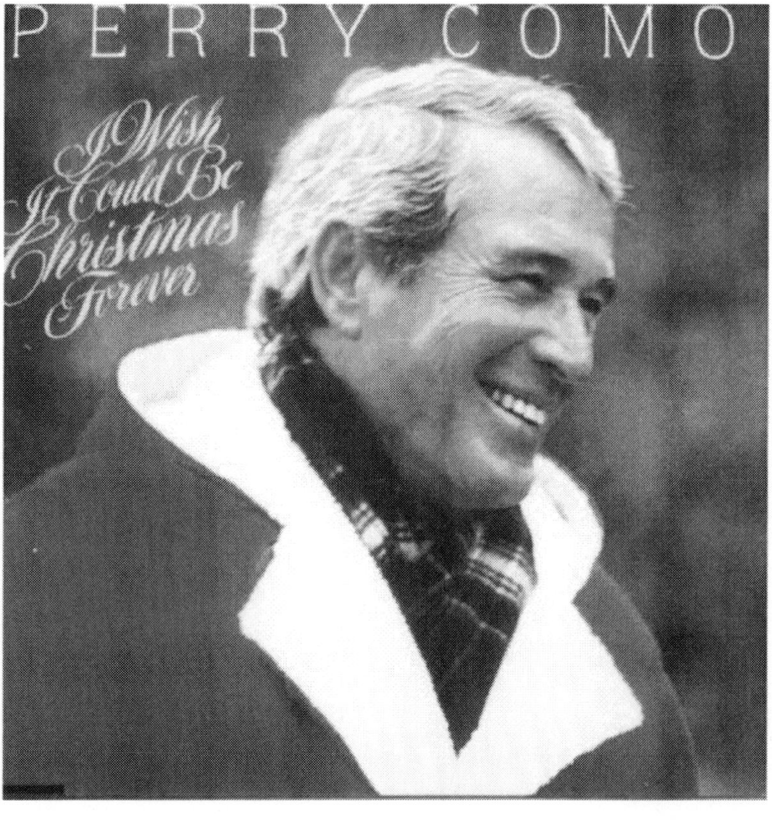
PERRY COMO
I Wish It Could Be Christmas Forever

PERRY COMO

June 10, 1997

Mr. Jack Ellsworth
President/General Manager
Radio Station WLIM
Woodside Avenue
Patchogue, L.I., N.Y. 11772

Dear Jack:

I just wanted to congratulate you on your fifty years in radio.

It's quite an accomplishment, and I hope that you will continue with your good work. We all need you and your music!

"Salute"
Perry

Letter from Perry Como

Photos, clippings from my private collection
Top left: Johnny Mince, top right Eubie Blake
Middle : Louis Armstrong
Bottom Left : Arthur Tracy, Bottom Right: Doris Day

Stories from the Stars

"Life will go on as long as there is someone to sing, to dance, to tell stories and to listen."   ~ Oren Lyons

Eubie Blake

In 1980 I was invited to emcee a jazz festival at Quinnipiac College in Hamden, Connecticut. Among the many dignitaries on hand were Dave Brubeck, Benny Goodman, Mrs. Louis Armstrong and famous song writer-pianist, Eubie Blake.

Following a dinner that preceded the concert, I had a chance to chat with Eubie, then well into his nineties. I told him how much I enjoyed his music especially "Memories of You" which I had been using as a theme song for my program "Memories in Melody." He laughed and said "You know Jack I really didn't write "Memories of You." Seeing my puzzled look he explained, "Do you remember Edward MacDowell's 'To A Wild Rose'?" I said I did, having heard it in my grade school music appreciation class. Eubie, smiling broadly, continued, "Well just hum that melody and you'll hear where I got the main theme for Memories of You. Anyway", he said "I'm glad you enjoy it!"

Louis Armstrong and Johnny Mince

Lucille Armstrong was also present at the Quinnipiac college affair. I was reminded of a story told to me by my old friend Johnny Mince, one of the greatest clarinet players of all time and a prominent member of Tommy Dorsey's famous band for six years. Johnny lived in Blue Point here on Long Island and he taught our sons, Gary and Glenn to play the clarinet and the saxophone. He also was our daughter Susan's flute teacher.

In his later years, Johnny was a member of Louis Armstrong's Allstars. After Louis Armstrong's death in 1971, Johnny told me about a visit he had with the legendary trumpet player. He started the story saying "If ever I wished I had a tape recorder...one day following a concert" he said "Louis called me into his little office and said 'John, I want you to know I really dig you man. You play so great and you are a beautiful cat. Them other cats is the band, they're just waitin' for 'ole pops to cut out so they can take over the band...but it ain't gonna happen. You aren't like them John. You are my man and I want you to know I really love you!"

Johnny left the room with tears in his eyes. "Imagine the great Louis Armstrong saying that to me! It's something I'll never forget."

Doris Day

During a meeting and brief interview with Doris Day in New York City, I found her to be very friendly and outgoing. She said she liked Califronia but always wanted to live in New England. I told her that she would love Long Island because there are some parts of Suffolk County which in season, are very similar to California. I asked about her favorite foods. She said, "I just love ice cream but I wonder if I would still like it served warm?" I then asked what was it about her career that gave her the most satisfaction? She quickly replied, "Meeting people like you who play our records and say such nice things!" She later said in conversation that she hated to watch her films. She explained, "I find myself thinking, 'Do I really look like that?' 'Did I say that?' I may have allayed her fears as she giggled when I told her that DJ Dan Ingram once said, "There is no Doris Day, no one sings that well, looks so gorgeous and can act too!"

Arthur Tracy

Once, while I was dining in a mid-town Manhattan restaurant, I spotted the legendary Arthur Tracy enjoying a meal. I smiled and waved to him. Realizing that I had recognized him, he immediately came right over to say hello! I said, "Who can forget your great hit!" Whereupon he burst into "Marta Rambling Rose of the Wildwood" The other diners stood up and applauded! He was well into his 80's at the time but his vice was loud and clear!

Part IV

Acclaim and Recognition

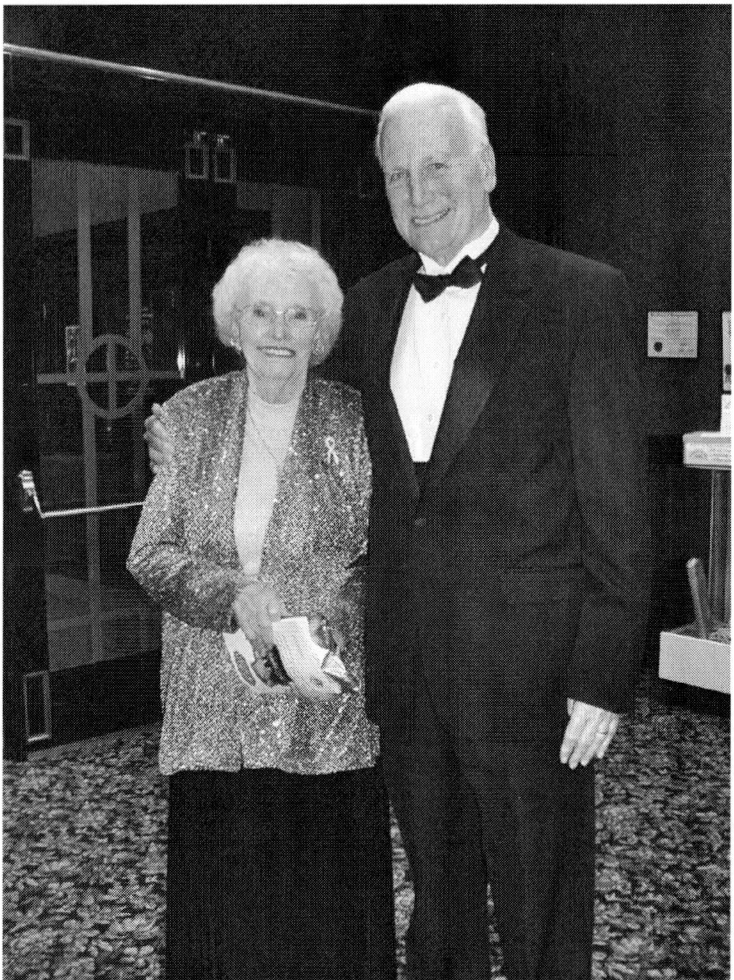

Jacks note:

(My family thought that these past articles should be included. Each one generously expresses some very kind words about my career!)

The Silver Fox

Written by Brian Curry
(Originally printed in "Garden City Life"- February 16th 1995)

When you meet him the words "style" "grace" and "class" come to mind. The handshake is firm and you're ushered into his office.

While the walls in his comfortable living room-like reception area are filled with accolades and testimonials to his many years of service to the community, his office reflects his music, his passion, indeed his true love. There are pictures with Frank Sinatra, Benny Goodman and Tommy Dorsey. These aren't those formal press-type photos with quickly scribbled autographs. Instead, there are personal notes from true friends, people with whom he shared the golden days of a time when popular music was pure quality.

He is Jack Ellsworth, a man who has graced the radio airwaves on Long Island for 40 + years. He started in college radio, moving on to stations in Newark and Providence before coming to WGSM (the first Long Island station) in early 1950. In the fall of 1951 he moved over to WALK where he spent over 30 years before buying WLIM.

WLIM was more than a radio station or a business venture for Jack. It was the home he built for his music. The music of composers like Gershwin, Porter and Berlin. Singers like Sinatra, Crosby and Peggy Lee. Bands like those of Miller and Goodman.

He built such a comfortable home for these people because he was with them during those heady days of the 30s and 40s, sharing a dream. "It really felt like a dream that would never end...we'd go from one show to another and there was always such great music," Mr. Ellsworth said between songs on his "Memories in Melody" morning show.

He was more than a disc jockey to the stars. He was their friend. They sensed a knowledge and, more importantly, a love for what they were trying to do. It's twice reflected in Sinatra's naming of Jack in his liner notes on his Columbia Records boxed set and in his station promos for his "old buddy." Bing Crosby gave one of his last interviews before he died to Mr. Ellsworth. And Benny Goodman spent his birthday at the station.

He admits feeling somewhat like a "dinosaur" but feels a need to keep this "golden era of popular music" alive. His wife Dot tells him once they're gone, that will be it, but for now he doesn't even think of retirement because he still loves playing the music.

So, Jack spins his songs and interweaves them with personal stories and you feel like you're at
the Paramount Theatre with a young crooner from Hoboken, New Jersey and in a way you are because the "Silver Fox" has taken you there.

***Since this article was written Jack has sold WLIM and is back at WALK AM 1370 on your dial, Tuesdays through Thursdays from 11 to 12 Noon with his familiar "Memories In Melody" and on "Sundays with the Sinatra" Show from 9 to 10 AM.

Memories in Melodies

By Betty Jane Welgand
(originally published in the Brookhaven Review)

There's a new kid on the block, spanking clean and raring to go. It's WLIM - 1580 on the AM dial in Patchogue, N.Y. Owners Jack Ellsworth, his wife, Dot, and George Drake, can't help bragging about their new offspring, and like the new parents they are, talk endlessly about their three month old baby.

The new station's easy listening format answers the needs of many radio listeners who are weary of hunting for more than rock and roll.

The staff, with voices as deep and velvety smooth as the plush new carpeting that runs the length and breadth of the spacious station, are, according to Ellsworth, "some of the finest broadcasters ever heard on Long Island."

Walking through the corridors of this station is like being led through The Looking Glass. People who were but disembodied voices on your radio soon become real.

One such person, Bob Dorian, a morning personality, also does all the station's specialized production work. Working on a Halloween promotional tape, he stands at a giant console which fills the small sound studio. Tapes squiggle, tape recorders hum, turntables spin and a large mixer blinks red-eyed lights. Dorian, the station's Wizard of Oz, moves from dials to switches with the agility of a John McEnroe on the courts at Wimbledon.

A man with a thousand voices, Dorian imitates first Frankenstein, then Igor, his helper. He cuts a tape using the voice of Petter Lorrie. "Radio," he says, "is the theatre of the mind. It lets your imagination come alive."

While Dorian mixes it up with Lorrie and Frankenstein, in the next studio Steve Roberts is broadcasting his noon 'til three program. His voice is smooth, like the records he plays. In his small sound studio surrounded by glass windows, the turntable spins and Robert Goulet sings, "The Moon is Yellow."

The selections for each show are taken from the station's large record library. "Every selection is hand-picked," said Dot Ellsworth, who helps her husband, Jack, choose his songs for his morning show, "Memories in Melody." According to Dot, who is Treasurer of the new station, WLIM can broadcast for over three months without repeating a song.

The news department is headed up by the station's vice-president, George Drake, who also hosts an early morning show. "This is no rip and read affair," claims Ellsworth "Every article is researched and then written up by each newscaster."

The station's large staff is a closely knit group, each doing a little bit of on-the-air work to selling advertising time. It is reminiscent of the old mom and pop store, where everyone worked and the business was their life.

"There's an old saying," said Ellsworth, a boyish smile lighting up his face, "every once in a while, a window opens, so you better jump through." He is referring to the big step of owning a radio station. "It's fantastic how listeners and sponsors have followed us over here at WLIM. Of course, we don't have everybody - there are still some funny hold outs." He tells a funny story of going to a "7-11" store one night after work to hear a pre-recorded show of his own on the store's radio. "I didn't want to say, 'Say that's my show fellas,' to the two young kids who were working behind the counter, so instead I said something like, 'What's that radio station you've got on?' preparing myself for the accolades. The kids looked at me and said, 'Gee, I don't know, the boss left it on, but it's gotta go'." Ellsworth grins, "You can't win 'em all folks!"

Jack Ellsworth to be Honored

By Chuck Anderson
(Excerpts reprinted with permission from the Long Island Advance, 1997)

Jack Ellsworth, known to friends and followers as "The Silver Fox," was sitting in his office at WLIM, reflecting on 50 years in the radio business. The walls were lined with plaques and certificates of appreciation, baseball and show business memorabilia, including at least five renderings of Frank Sinatra and artwork executed by various grandchildren. The fourth wall was covered with an ocean scene, waves breaking on a beach, perhaps reminding Ellsworth of his affection for Long Island.

"Radio has changed since I started working here," Ellsworth said, "When I started on the island there were four radio stations. Now there are 31 plus cable television which replicates a lot of radio services."

Ellsworth was born Ellsworth Adee Shiebler on June 13, 1922 in Flatbush, Brooklyn. He graduated from Brooklyn Academy in 1941, just before the attack on Pearl Harbor. After serving as a marine sergeant during World War II, Ellsworth attended Brown University in Providence, R.I. where he got his start in radio and changed his name from Ellsworth Shiebler to Jack Ellsworth. An aspiring actor, he came close to signing a contract with MGM. (Well known journalist and gossip columnist Walter Winchell wrote, "Ex-Marine Jack Ellsworth is MGM's latest threat to the sleep of American womanhood.")

Forty-six years ago Ellsworth came to Long Island and since then his daily show, "Memories in Melody," has been the longest continuous program in the area. By 1975, he was the station manager of WALK and considers his leadership of the flagship station of Island Broadcasting from 1975 until 1980 as one of the highlights of his career.

In 1981, Ellsworth purchased his own station and took his loyal listeners and staunch sponsors with him to WLIM, where he has carved out a substantial niche in the radio audience.

Ellsworth credits his wife Dorothy with much of his success. Dorothy "Dot" Ellsworth was recently named "Woman of the Year" by the Advance and in 1989 she was honored as "Woman of the Year in Communication" by the Town of Brookhaven. Of his wife, Ellsworth said, "She does a fabulous job and really keeps the station running smoothly."

In addition to his encyclopedic knowledge of music, another reason for Ellsworth's success is probably because he is the quintessential fan. He said, "There are many stars that I truly admire. I got to meet and spend time with Bing Crosby, Frank Sinatra, Dick Powell and Benny Goodman. I told Bing once, 'Bing, all my life you've been my idol.' He said, 'Jack, you've got to aim higher than that'."

Evidently, Jack Ellsworth has aimed high enough. He is on the executive board of the Suffolk County Council of the Boy Scouts of America, on the advisory board at Brookhaven Memorial Hospital, a former president and legion of honor member of the Kiwanis Club, and president, for two years, of the Bellport Chamber of Commerce. (Dot was also president for many years) In 1985 he was the recipient of the South Country Lions Club

Man of the Year award, the Arts Achievement award presented by the Babylon Town Council on the Arts, and The Boy Scouts Good Deed award. Several years ago, he was named Humanitarian of the Year by the Knights of Columbus, and became a life member of the Suffolk County Police Association. In 1989, he was honored by Suffolk Community College for "distinguished contributions to broadcasting on Long Island."

According to Ellsworth, his greatest achievement is his family. He and his wife Dorothy have two sons, Gary and Glenn and a daughter, Susan. They also have seven grandchildren; Jillian, Hayden, Alice, Michael, Elissa, Anne and Matthew (Christa and Jackson soon followed in 1997 and 2000 respectively)

This year, (1997) Jack Ellsworth's family and the staff of WLIM will honor his fifty years of broadcasting at a dinner dance held at the Bellport Country Club, with a lavish buffet and four hours of dancing to Ben Grisafi's big band.

Bing Crosby would approve.

Paul Harvey
The Rest of the Story

Everyone is familiar with Paul Harvey's famous radio program "The Rest of the Story." His familiar opening words were... "Hello fellow Americans, This is Paul Harvey. You know what the news is...in a moment, you're going to hear the rest of the story." Here's Paul Harvey's tribute to Jack Ellsworth while he was at WLIM:

    Okay, so here's the question: How do you describe a station that for 20 years has remained completely dedicated to both its format and listeners? Well, to start off, it takes a special kind of radio personality to make it happen. This person has to have a rock solid background in broadcasting and should know Long Island like a book. He must have the ability to keep his ship (or radio station if you prefer) 'steady as it goes,' even through the most difficult of times. It must be a warm person who cares not only about his station's listeners but personally remains active within the local community as well. I can only think of one person who completely fits this description and made everything happen. That person is Long Island's very own Jack Ellsworth, better known within the radio community as the "Silver Fox."

The year was 1970. I was 13 years old when my family moved from Jackson Heights to Long Island. Our kitchen radio was set to one station, WALK 97.5 FM, which is where I first heard the Jack Ellsworth program. Our entire family really enjoyed Jack's splendid taste in big band and popular standards music, along with his warm personality and charming on-air sense of humor.

For many years to follow, I grew up listening to the Silver Fox. From witty news comments about big band artists to winter school closings, my family was hooked on Jack's program. I also learned a lot about the Big Bands from listening to him!

Years, later, we heard a familiar voice on another station. You guessed it...The Silver Fox was back, this time on WLIM! And....let's not forget the driving force behind the man who made everything possible at WLIM. I am talking about Jack's lovely and highly talented wife Dottie who, for over 20 years was the station's vice-president and general manager.

Both Jack and Dottie went on to make WLIM the premier station for Long Island's favorite music...American Popular Standards and Big Bands!

(Paul Harvey, 1918-2009 was a conservative American radio broadcaster for the ABC Radio Networks. He broadcast News and Comment on weekday mornings and mid-days, and at noon on Saturdays, as well as his famous 'The Rest of the Story" segments. His listening audience was estimated, at its peak, at 24 million people a week. Paul Harvey News was carried on 1,200 radio stations, 400 Armed Forces Network stations and 300 newspapers. His broadcasts and newspaper columns have been reprinted in the Congressional Record more than those of any other commentator.)

WLIM Tribute

An online site By Rick Hall   www.wackradio.com/wlim

For over 20 years, Jack and Dotty were the proud owners and operators of WLIM 1580 in Patchogue, New York... a station which previously held the call letters: WPAC. I never thought I would meet the person who charmed my entire family on the air with his great choice of music selections. I am happy to say, that day came in December 1996 when I was introduced to Jack and Dotty by my close friend Mike Erickson (WFAN) and long time WLIM On-Air Personality and operations coordinator Bob Stern.

Bob and I share many common interests. In particular, we are fascinated with vintage recordings and movies. Thanks to Bob and Mike, I was introduced to Jack and I must say, it was truly an honor meeting the Silver Fox in person for the very first time. We all sat down in his office and started talking about radio and all the famous recording artists he personally knew. I was completely taken back when he showed me a picture of him posing with Glenn Miller (the photo is located on the upper left side of the main air studio wall). Jack was also personal friends with Dick Powell. In fact, Jack and Dick were considered pen pals and kept in close contact with each other for many years.

Most impressive is the extensive music library at WLIM. This the heart of the programming and what sets this station apart from all the others. You name it, WLIM had it and played it!

When atmospheric conditions were perfect, this station could actually be heard thousands of miles away. That's right, specifically Nova Scotia. I was at the station with Bob Stern one evening when Mike walked in with a QSL letter and a cassette from a DXer in Nova Scotia who recorded about 10 minutes of Mike's show and requested a reception confirmation. I believe the receiver used in the DX which captured Mike's WLIM station identification announcement was a Grundig.

For one truly interesting piece of information about Jack Ellsworth's past radio history deserves to be mentioned. Early in his career, while working at WALK FM, Jack was going through a pile of air-check tapes submitted by Disc-Jockeys seeking employment. He came across one tape, which back then, had an unfamiliar name and voice on it. Having a well 'tuned' ear for prospective talent, Jack wasted no time hiring the 'unknown' person on the tape. Today, that person is credited as being the all time #1 air-personality and voice-over artist in the broadcast industry, both here in the USA and throughout the entire world. His name: Dan Ingram.

I would like to take this opportunity to personally thank Jack and Dotty Ellsworth for allowing me to be a small part of WLIM's family of friends and for bringing many years of great music, happiness and splendid memories to their audience. I don't think I have ever met a nicer pair of people in the entire Long Island Radio Community. Thanks again for all the wonderful memories and best of luck to you both! This page on my site is dedicated to you.
Signed, Your buddy Rick Hall

To Hear Jack Ellsworth's Original First Air-Check Transcription Demo from 1947- Go to www.wackradio.com/wlim

Special thanks from Dot and I to Rick Hall for keeping this internet tribute page up all of these years!)

Jack Ellsworth Is Back and WALK's Got Him

by Dick Grudens

First there was Marconi, then crystal sets, followed by New York City's WNEW with Martin Block. Then, here on Long Island there was a fellow, a former U.S. Marine Corps Combat Correspondent by the name of Jack Ellsworth, who started his disc jockey radio show "Memories in Melody" on radio station WALK in Patchogue and held rein for some thirty years.

Well, Top 40 stuff filtered therein and Jack, his wife Dot, and their Newscaster partner George Drake, picked up their 78's and started a new radio station called WLIM, also in Patchogue. They kept the same format of Big Band music and invited some big name visitors to the station, names like Larry Elgart, Ray Anthony, the great Benny Goodman (who stayed all day) and the entire Glenn Miller Orchestra with Larry O'Brien. Jack had already interviewed Sinatra and Crosby earlier, and they both contributed soundies for the new station's promotions.

Upon Jack's 50th Anniversary in 1997 as a disc jockey, Sinatra wrote him, saying: "We've traveled many musical miles together, my friend. I am delighted to send cheers and bravos to you on 50 marvelous years of championing our kind of music.
"As I raise a glass of bubbly, I thank you for your generous support of my career --- you're a good man."

Back in 1941 Jack's story began:

"I received a phone call from popular jock Art Ford, who later had an all-night show on WNEW called the Milkman's Matinee. Art was running a Bing Crosby show on station WBNX in the Bronx, and he had heard I had a great Crosby record collection. He asked me to bring it up to his studio. I was a teenager and very impressionable. I was thrilled to be a radio show guest."
Jack became a frequent visitor on Art's show, talking about all the greats. Smitten with the radio bug while at Brown University in 1947, Jack hosted a show on campus, using his Art Ford credentials. There was no monetary compensation, but he thoroughly enjoyed spinning the 78s that so influenced his life.

"I applied for a disc jockey job with a station that had a WNEW style format and got the job. After three years of top ratings, I accepted a similar position at WVNJ in Newark, New Jersey, and in 1950 I heard about a station in Huntington, Long Island called WGSM, and obtained a similar job there. A year later I went to work for WALK.

Jack met his wife Dot in 1951 and married her in November. She had been a legal secretary. They settled in Bellport and he began work at WALK, and in 1963 was promoted to station manager. In 1975 he became President, General Manager and CEO. In 1980 WALK was sold. Jack, Dot and George Drake started WLIM.

During his 30 years at WALK Jack interviewed many heavyweights like Doris Day, Dick Haymes, Les Paul and Mary Ford as well as Sinatra and Crosby, among others.

"There is a uniqueness in radio," Jack says, "When I put on Glenn's 'Moonlight Serenade,' I could cry from its solemn beauty.

People can close their eyes and take themselves back to the time in their lives when they first heard the classic tune. It's great therapy, and always pleasant listening, unlike the frenetic music of today."

Well, now Jack has been back at WALK, 1370 AM with his same show "Memories in Melody" for a few years now. I have spent some time with Jack on the air being interviewed for some of my books. One day I brought the one and only Jerry Vale to the station as a surprise for Jack while he was on the air. Well, he jumped up and hugged Jerry and turned the show over to him and his music. He had never met Jerry Vale, but had talked to him on the phone many times. It was a great reunion of sorts and everyone at the station was very happy to witness the meeting of two giants of music.

So, Jack is back home at WALK where he first started. Jack is over eighty now and you would never know it. Dot is over 21 and still sets the music for the show and guides Jack by programming titles and future formats. They are a great team. Dot is Jack's CEO. And Jack just loves it.

In early 2003, I invited Jack to a book signing in Stony Book with Bing's wife, Kathryn. Jack brought his photo collection and showed it to Kathryn who really enjoyed seeing it. It was the first time they had met. At the podium Jack introduced Kathryn who graciously sang a song in tribute to Bob Hope who had passed away just a few days earlier.

Day by day Jack Ellsworth continues his music. Just today, November 23, 2009, Jack played some Glenn Miller favorites, three Woody Herman tunes with Woody singing "It Must Be Jelly, ' Cause Jam Don't Shake Like That," and a few Buddy Clark favorites including "South America - Take it Away." There was also an opening selection with Count Basie, and always a Ella Fitzgerald and Nat "King" Cole piece played during each show.

You had better tune in 10-12 daily to 1370 AM radio.
(Now 11-12 Tue-Thurs)
If you don't, you are really missing something.
God bless Jack and Dot Ellsworth and "Memories in Melody."

Jacks note: Dick Gruden is a respected Big Band author and has written over 14 books about the subject covering vocalists, musicians, band leaders, arrangers, and associates, including his best seller Star Dust - The Bible of the Big Bands, a book with over 700 pages and 650 terrific photographs. Dick has been kind enough to mention me in many of his books and share his wealth of knowledge as a guest on my show. I greatly appreciate his friendship …and also his advice while I was writing this book.

Part V
Recollections

My son, Gary and I taking a stroll together, talking and reminiscing as we often do.

Whatever Happened To...?

"We do not remember days; we remember moments."
~ Cesare Pavese

    Even though not all memories have to be associated with melodies, I debated as to whether or not I should include this chapter in the book. Like some of the other chapters, it is excerpted from one of my newspaper columns from some years back but it is not about music. The memories in this chapter are things that maybe only people who are older than seventy will recall. These are items and events that unlike melodies which linger, are now mostly long gone. I ultimately decided that if something mentioned here brings some happiness to even one person or causes recollection of a pastime, even an item or place long forgotten, it is worth it.

    Isn't it amazing that some of our richest memories come from the simplest of details? For example, how many of us are left who remember getting a coal delivery to our home and the sound of the coal sliding down the chute into the basement coal bin? Who doesn't remember with utmost fondness the milk delivered to our doors and the cream frozen at the top of the bottles left on the doorstep of cold winter mornings?

I wonder how many remember the "I Cash Clothes" man, the knife and scissors sharpener, the organ grinder with his monkey and before refrigerators how the ice man was a regular visitor?

While reminiscing I started thinking about some of the great five cent candy treats that have long since disappeared. How I used to love to munch on Kerr's Butterscotch, Mary Jane's, Bonomos' Turkish Taffy, Mason Mints, Nestles Sportsman's Bracer (rich dark chocolate) Black Crows Licorice Drops, Walnettos, Forever Yours, Clark Bars, Y & S Licorice Drops, and Twenty Five Carat, delicious chocolate with a pecan in the middle, all wrapped in gold foil.

In Brooklyn, I loved the crumpets and cream puffs at Cushman's Bakery and the coffee cake, crumb buns and eclairs from Ebingers. How about the home delivery bakery companies like Dugan's, Larsens and Krug?

Then there were the grocery stores of yesteryear. Remember the James Butler Stores, Thomas Roulston, Royal Scarlet Stores, Daniel Reeves, Merit Farms Dairy Stores and other small independent grocers. When did the last Bohack store close? Wasn't there an A & P in your neighborhood?

On the shelves of these and other grocery stores were products that have now disappeared. Great foods like Pabstet Cheese, Liederkranz Cheese, Rath's pure pork sausage, Richardson and Robbins boned chicken, G. Washington Coffee, Cocomalt, Silvercup, Tip Top or Bond Breads and a breakfast cereal called "Pep." I remember a cake mix called "Cuplets." You added an egg and milk and you could bake eight delicious cupcakes!

It may seem silly to even recall laundry detergents and such but for some reason, the scents and sights of even these mundane items are indelible in our minds. Long gone now from stores is Rinso, Silver Dust, Halo Shampoo and Lux Flakes. I also seem to recall a product called Oxol, which may have been a laundry bleach. My mom used to buy it. My grandmother loved Hinds

Honey and Almond Cream. There was Fels Naptha Soap, Kirkman's soap and Burma Shave. Maybe somewhere these items are still available!

Consider the following magazines, some long established, now no longer published. Colliers. Woman's Home Companion, Flair, The American Magazine, Liberty, Look, Delineator, Saturday Evening Post, St. Nicolas, Judge, The American Boy, Boy's Life, Scribners, Literary Digest, Farm and Fireside, Pictorial Review, Pic, Coronet, Pageant and Radio Times. I so clearly remember the movie magazines such as Modern Screen, Silver Screen, Photoplay, Motion Pictures, Film Fun, Bally Hoo and the original Life Magazine which stopped being published in 1936 and gave way to the more recent Life which was more of a news magazine.

There are the now defunct newspapers many will recall from the New York area, The NY World, The Globe, The NY Sun, The Daily Mirror, The Herald Tribune, The American, The Journal American, The Brooklyn Eagle, Times Union. the Long Island Press and the Suffolk Sun.

Today, sports cards are still available but does anyone remember Indian Cards? They also came with a strip of gum. I acquired quite a large collection. We used to play a game of flipping cards, sort of a matching heads or tails idea. One day my younger brother "borrowed" my collection and I lost them all. I had a hard time forgiving him for that one.

Memories come flooding back when I recall the days spent at the soda fountain. I can still see the extra glass of a malted or a milk shake in the shaker. I remember cherry cokes and "Nibble-A-Nab" for a nickel. Then there were the greatest games of childhood ever. Hop Scotch, Potsy, Ring-A-Levio, Street Hockey, Stoop Ball, Red Rover, Kick the Can, Giant Steps, Territory, Mumbly Peg, One-A-Cat and Bar-Hi Bouncer Punch Balls. No one can forget good old Hide and Seek. Remember yelling "Ally Ally in Free" (or "Ally Ally Oxen Free") How sad that children don't play outside today as much as they used to. Then there were the crazy things we used to say as kids, "Step on a crack, break your mothers back," "That's two for flinching" and "Takes one to know one." Of course there were the things we would rather not remember like the crazy bets and dares to be stupid. I remember walking on the edge of the roof outside our third floor window and on the narrow ledge over the Brighton Beach subway line. What was I thinking?!

Lastly, how wonderful and such a special part of childhood were the comic strips of yesteryear? Some that I remember well are "The Katzenjammer Kids," "Major Hoople," "Hairbreadth Harry," "Smilin' Jack," "Jane Arden," "Connie," "Joe Palooka," Smitty," and "Bringing Up Father." How about "Jiggs and Maggie," "The Gumps," "Ella Cinders," "Apple Mary," "Moon Mullins," "Tillie the Toiler" and "Little Nemo."

Will the children born in the last ten-forty years have similar great memories? Surely there are Disney movies, cartoons and games that have been entertaining and will likely be remembered with fondness. Shows like Sesame Street and even computer and video games for children will even one day be recalled as something of yesteryear. My grandchildren today, are already remarking that cartoons are not the same and that candy and chips packaging have gotten drastically smaller since they were very little.... only ten-fifteen years ago!

All of us who have lived through the middle to the end of the 1900's recall with joy the early quality TV series, a list that could go on forever. We know that life is changing dramatically, all we have to do is see the change in technology every year and listen to the news.

Whether we are nine years old or ninety, like yours truly, we all need to cherish the moment, appreciate simple pleasures and look around at what we probably take for granted. When we do this, we will always be able to look back at the good memories of the past with no regret. We should try to overlook and move beyond any bad memories we have. (And we all have them)
Maybe today life is easier with large screen T.V.'s, elaborate computers and cell phones and so many "modern conveniences" but doesn't it sometimes seem a bit too much and a bit too easy? Should whatever we want be so available? We live in a time when instant gratification is the name of the game. Wasn't it better when somehow we had to look and work a little harder for our

pleasures? Didn't we appreciate things more? Weren't we happier and less stressed?

In today's world, when times are wearying, it helps to sometimes close our eyes and recall what made us smile on a day long ago. Despite the stress of the present, if we take just a minute to reminisce and recall a simpler, happier day or moment, it is sure to make us smile again.

Our four grandchildren, Michael, Elissa, Matthew and Christa, gathered around an old radio, as they re-create a 1940's scene for a Christmas Card.
Photo: Susan Elise Shiebler Photography

Radio Recollections

"I like radio better than television because if you make a mistake on radio they don't know. You can make anything on the radio." ~ Phil Rizzuto

Radio has been perfectly called the "Theatre of the Mind." As you listened, you conjured up your own mental images of the music, the characters and the scenes. (Is television really an improvement over the pictures in your own imagination?) The history of radio is rich and extensive. From shows to broadcasts, from sports to interviews. how many stories have we heard from grandparents about the joy of family time as everyone use to gather around the radio in the evenings?

Even the great musicians in this book were known for their wonderful radio broadcasts.

Glenn Miller's most frequent broadcasts were from the Cafe Rouge at New York's Pennsylvania Hotel. Tommy Dorsey could often be heard form the Hollywood Palladium Ballroom. Benny Goodman's earliest remote broadcasts were from The Congress Hotel in Chicago. Frankie Carle was heard from the Mark Hopkins Hotel in San Francisco. Most of the big band broadcasts were from New York City. We heard Artie Shaw from the Hotel Lincoln, Gene Krupa from the Astor Hotel Roof Garden, Harry James and Count Basie from the Riverboat at the lower level of the Empire State building.

There were numerous other early radio shows, most long forgotten and not even listed in the few existing radio memorabilia books. Those that linger in my memory include: Just Plain Bill, Campana Serenade with Dick Powell and Martha Tilton, Easy Aces, Vox Pop, Information Please and Kay Kayser's Kollege of Musical Knowledge.

Who remembers the original John B. Gambling Show? For me, none of the successors had the same appeal. His live music and banter with the cast were extremely entertaining. Then, there was a long list of memorable radio favorites: *Lux Radio Theatre, The Whistler, Murder at Midnite, Inner Sanctum, Suspense, Bob & Ray, Mr. Keen, Tracer of Lost Persons, Coast to Coast on a Bus, The Singing Lady, Let's Pretend, Galen Drake's Housewive's Protective League, The Carnation Contented Hour* with Buddy Clark and Percy Faith's orchestra. *Tune up Time* with Andre Kostelanetz's orchestra, *Good News of 1940, Stan Lomax's Sports, Ford Frick's Sports, Red Barber* ("In the Catbird Seat"), and Al Helfer's Brooklyn Dodgers play-by-play, Arch MacDonald's NY Giants games ("Right Down Broadway") and Mel Allen's Yankee games ("How About That"?)

How many of the famous early announcers and newscasters can you recall? Here are a few names that come to mind: Ken Carpenter, Don Wilson, Harry Von Zell, Robert Trout, Norman Brokenshire, H.V. Kaltenborn, Boake Carter, Gabriel Heatter, Graham MacNamee, Tiny Ruffner, Jimmy Wallington, Floyd Gibbons, Ken Niles, Andre Baruch, Glenn Riggs, Bill Hay, Ed Herlihy, Hugh James, Milton Cross, Bert Wayne, Bert Parks, Ken Roberts, Bill Abernathy, Larry Bruff, Paul Douglas, Stan Shaw, Martin Block, Paul Brenner, Art Ford, Jerry Marshall, Ted Husing,

Larry Keating, Jim Ameche, Dan Seymour, Bill Goodwin, Phil Goudling, Basil Ruysdale and who can forget Mr. Anthony and his sad guests.

While I was writing a column for a local newspaper, I had considerable response to my articles on old radio shows. We dug into our "Memories" files and came up with some titles and a few words associated with each program. How many do you remember?

> The Mysterious Traveler
> (A journey into the strange and terrifying)
>
> The Jimmy Durante Show
> (Goodnight, Mrs. Calabash.........)
>
> The Falcon
> (Two-fisted detective adventures)
>
> X Minus One
> (The adult science fiction program)
>
> Valiant Lady
> (A brave woman and her brilliant but unstable husband)
>
> Life Can Be Beautiful
> (Known to those in the know as "Elsie Beebee")
>
> Boston Blackie
> (Friend to those who have no friends)
>
> Uncle Don
> (No, he never said it)
>
> The Guiding Light
> (Still shining until just last year)
>
> Can You Top This?
> (With Harry Hershfield, Joe Laurie, Jr. & Senator Ford)

Tom Corbett, Space Cadet
(Roaring rockets to far-flung stars)

Major Bowes' Original Amateur Hour
("All right, all right!")

Here's Morgan
("Good evening, anybody")

True Detective Mysteries
("$1000 for information leading to......")

Stella Dallas
(A drama of mother-love and sacrifice, and tears, tears, tears)

Grand Central Station
(Where the world meets)

Lights Out
(The better to scare you)

Melody Ranch
("Back in the saddle again")

Mr. District Attorney
(Champion of the people)

One Man's Family
(And his bewildering offspring)

The Story of Dr. Kildare
(The man in white)

Nick Carter, Master Detective
(Most famous manhunter of them all)

Hop Harrigan
(America's ace of the airways)

It Pays to Be Ignorant
(Who is buried in Grant's tomb?)

Pepper Young's Family
(The story of your friends, the Youngs)

I Love a Mystery
(Jack, Doc and Reggie)

The Bill Stern Sports Newsreel
(The Colgate shave cream man)

The Phil Harris-Alice Faye Show
("That's what I like about the South……")

Lorenzo Jones
(And his wife Belle)

Captain Midnight
(And the shake-up mug)

The Green Hornet
(With Kato and the Black Beauty Helping Out)

Richard Diamond, Private Eye
(Starring Dick Powell as the Singing Private Eye)

Ma Perkins
(America's Mother of the Airwaves)

Bulldog Drummond
("Out of the fog…..out of the night")

Red Ryder
(And Little Beaver)

Big Sister
("R…I…N…S…O")

Terry and the Pirates
(Adventures in the Orient)

Let Yourself Go
(With Ziegfeld's biggest folly, Milton Berle)

Young Dr. Malone
(Featuring Sandy Becker)

The FBI in Peace and War
(They always got their man)

The First Nighter Program
(The little theatre off Times Square)

The Adventures of Sam Spade, Detective
(Hello sweetheart)

Dr. I.Q.
(The mental banker with that lady on the balcony)

The Fat Man
(Weight…..237 pounds, fortune…..danger)

The March of Time
(Narrated by "The Voice of Doom")

The Goldbergs
(Yoo hoo...Is anybody home?)

Young Widder Brown
(Ellen Brown vs. Dr. Anthony Loring)

John's Other Wife
(In reality, his secretary)

Life with Luigi
(Played by Irishman J. Carroll Naish)

The Adventures of Sherlock Holmes
(Basil Rathbone & Nigel Bruce)

The Shadow of Fu Manchu
(Still eluding Sir Nayland Smith)

Hoofbeats, Starring Buck Jones
(Buck always eats Grape Nut Flakes)

The Chamber Music Society of Lower Basin Street
(Music of the Three B's)

Bobby Benson and the B-Bar-B Riders
(The Cowboy Kid himself)

Hal Kemp on the Air for Griffin
(A date with an angel)

The Raleigh and Kool Cigarette Program
(With Tommy Dorsey)

Sergeant Preston of the Yukon
(And his wonder dog King)

Jimmy Fiddler in Hollywood
(Latest lowdown on the big names)

Front Page Farrell
(A newspaper man and his wife)

David Harum
(Kindly little country philosopher)

Blondie
(Dagwood, Daisy and the pups)

Fitch Bandwagon
(Use your head, save your hair)

Scattergood Baines
(Country bumpkin triumphant over city slickers)

The Adventures of Philip Marlow
(Crime's most deadly enemy)

The Abbot & Costello Show
(Heyyyyyy Abbott!)

When a Girl Marries
(Dedicated to everyone who has ever been in love)

The Red Skelton Program
(And that mean little kid)

    I have often closed my own radio show "Memories in Melody" with two instructions, "Do something nice for someone today" and "Get involved." I hope the advice that I have also tried to live, has somewhere, somehow left a lasting impression. I have always wanted to bring the joy of great melodies that will create lasting memories. I hope I have done that in some small way as well.

    I am extremely proud of my friendship with so many show business greats, all mentioned in this book. They have enriched my life in countless ways and I have come a long way from that music-filled bedroom of a young boy in Brooklyn. I have been truly blessed to have had so many "Memories in Melody!"

As one of my old favorites, American radio personality Ben Bernie used to say,

"And now the time has come to lend thine ears to au revoir, pleasant dreams."

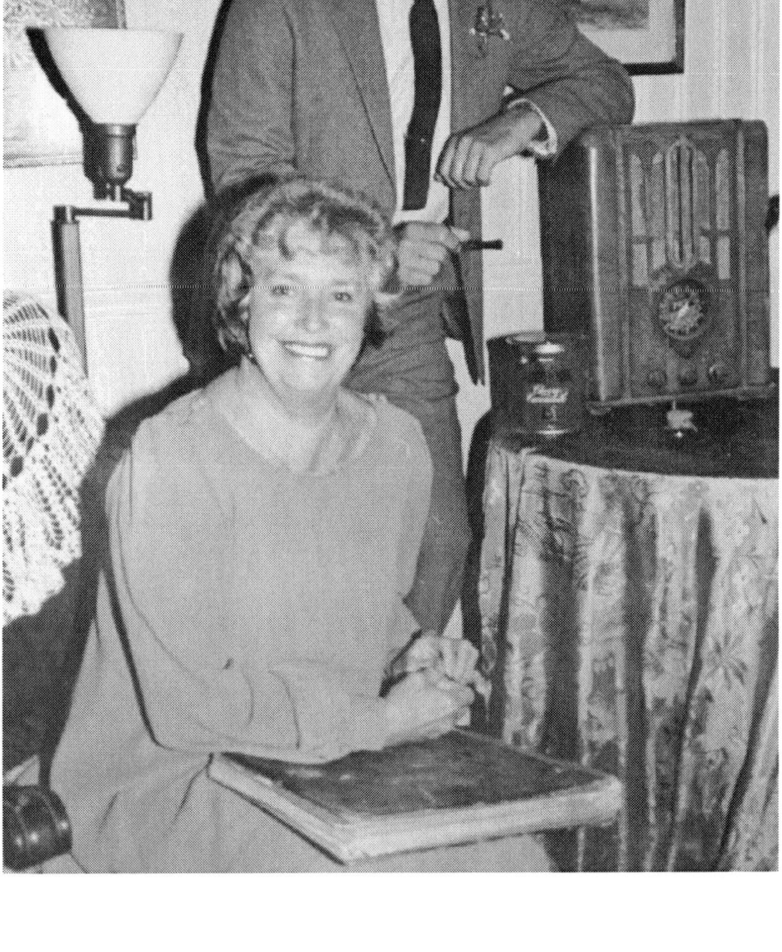

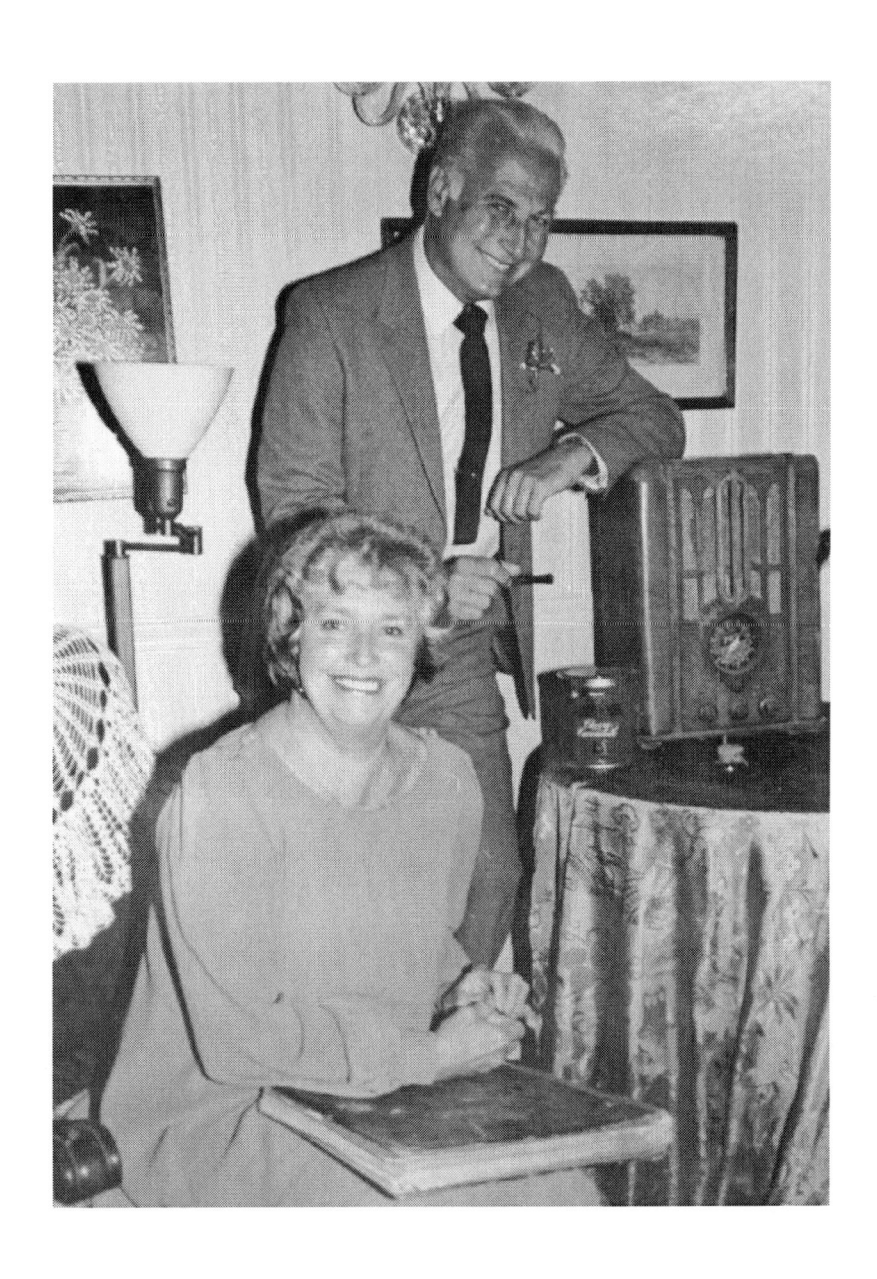